Where Mercy and Truth Meet: Homeless Women of Wheeler Speak

Editor
Darolyn "Lyn" Jones

Book design and layout
Michael Baumann

Student editors
Rita Mitchell & Nikki Wilkes

Volunteer editors
Barbara McLaughlin & Jessica Mayo

Cover art
Andrea Boucher

Photography
Giovanna "Joanne" Mandel

Where Mercy and Truth Meet:

Homeless Women of Wheeler Speak

Edited by Darolyn "Lyn" Jones

ISBN: 978-0-9849501-8-8

©2015 INwords Publications, publishing division
of the Indiana Writers Center

INwords Publications

c /o Indiana Writers Center

PO Box 30407

Indianapolis, IN 46230

www.indianawriters.org

Where Mercy and Truth Meet:
Homeless Women of Wheeler Speak

Edited by Darolyn "Lyn" Jones

INwords Publications
Indianapolis, Indiana

INwords PUBLICATIONS
PRESENTED BY THE **INDIANA WRITERS CENTER**

With Support From:

Allen Whitehall Clowe's Charitable

Foundation, Inc.

ARTSCOUNCIL
AND THE CITY OF INDIANAPOLIS

INDIANA WRITERS CENTER

INDIANA ARTS
COMMISSION

Where Mercy and Truth Meet: Homeless Women of Wheeler Speak

Mercy and truth are met together;
righteousness and peace have kissed each other.
Truth shall spring out of the earth; and
righteousness shall look down from heaven.

~Psalm 85:10-11

This collection is dedicated to the brave
and beautiful Women of Wheeler who
live and speak the truth. May Mercy
and Peace always be Yours.

Editor's Note
Darolyn "Lyn" Jones

I have been intrigued with memoir all of my life. I grew up with stories. My family never ran out of them, and I loved listening to them. I grew up hard, so when I became a writer, my life, like theirs, also became my stories. But instead of telling them, I write them.

When we think of stories, we might think of fiction, but the stories I write and the stories I edit are true. Memoirists don't have to invent characters, scene, dialogue, or plot. They just have to remember and bring those people, places, events, and words back to life on the page. Truth is always stranger — and much more interesting– than fiction. I tell my writers to tell your truth, uncover and discover your story, speak loud and proud of who you are and what you have lived. When I joined the Indiana Writers Center in 2004, I was asked to take writing out of the center. To take writing out to voices who deserve to be heard, deserved to be read.

I've always believed that the best memoirs are those written by an ordinary person who has experienced something extraordinary and has a story worth telling. Our Memoir Project at the Center was designed to help people of all ages and background to tell their stories. We based our mission under the axiom that that everybody has a story worth telling.

At the Indiana Writers Center, our goal has always been to capture the everyman's or in this case, the everywoman's story. At the Indiana Writers Center, we have now partnered with over 30 different community partners and served over 1,000 individuals, helping those who live on the fringe, who are marginalized, write their life.

This summer we were honored to partner with Wheeler Mission Ministries Center for Women and Children. Wheeler Mission is a historic and established homeless shelter for women and men in Indianapolis, Indiana. Their vision and mission is to provide programs, goods, and services for the homeless and poor in need. They also offer an addiction recovery program. We met with a group of homeless women twice a week for eight weeks for several hours and helped them write and tell their stories of struggle, heartbreak, and hope.

We fulfilled our mission to "nurture, educate, inspire, connect and support a diverse writing community" by supporting the publication of this anthology, *Where Mercy and Truth Meet: Homeless Women of Wheeler Speak.*

Barbara Kazanjian, a volunteer with the Memoir Project at the Indiana Writers Center's captures what it was like to write with the women at the Mission:

> We start a process akin to "just hangin," waiting for women with notebooks to collect. There is some coming and going. It's never the same way twice. Snacks are put out in the process of gathering, and that attracts attention of women who are curious, but hesitant to join.
>
> Sometimes someone drops in who wants to tell some of her story, rather than write it. Sisters of the Oral Tradition are accepted, but stongly encouraged to write. The writing here has a purpose—writing stories for deepening and preserving a sense of wholeness.
>
> Rarely do we see our stories and ourselves in the positive light of our courage and strength to overcome and move ahead through extreme and daunting circumstances. Much more likely we feel shame, failure, and are

aware of the harsh judgments of society. The most beautiful aspect for me of a creative community is to see the sense of self-worth bud, and then blossom in the faces of each other.

The stories are deep, harsh—sad. Yet, filled with making the best with what light is available in very dark places. In spite and because of this, the community is filled with humor--that ability to laugh at one's self without making a joke of one's self. Crying happens too— without self-pity—but with sorrow and regret. So much support is given and received in this intimate circle of sharing those deepest places in any give heart. Love in the tangible sense of friendship and Godly Presence completes the bond of making memories, by sharing memories.

The women in this special collection write about what they remember, what they have lost, what they dream of, and how they have ended up at, but have also found hope to begin again —at Wheeler.

This is an imperfect anthology. The stories are fragmented. They start and stop and may or may not start again. The chapters are uneven. Some women filled notebooks, like Valerie, and some wrote vignettes and poetry like Chandra. There is a blending of genres—a poem appears in the middle of an essay. Parts are unpolished. I don't edit out voice. Some wrote about best days instead of hard days. There are eight chapters, eight women who wrote multiple memoirs that were arranged either thematically or chronologically. Sandwiched between those chapters, you will find what I refer to as interludes, shorter pieces written by women who came once or who only wanted to write down one story.

And, finally, read reflections from our volunteers who wrote with and to the women.

Another choice we included regarding the design of this book is the placement of margins. Because the women in this anthology are homeless, they represent a marginalized population. When we write in the margins, we are not part of the text, but instead are responding as an outsider. We wanted the book to visually represent a different way of thinking regarding margins and the marginalized; therefore, our interior margins are larger. Typical books have larger outside margins where the main text often bleeds into the fold. We have moved our margins to the inside. The women's words are prominently pushed to the outside, to the fringe where they exist, and you have been invited inside to read about the most intimate details of their lives. In the interior margins, you are welcome to respond, to reflect, to recall your own memories and write them, even hide them in the fold. bell hooks, well-known feminist, writer, educator, and activist explains that a position of marginality presents itself as not a "site of deprivation," but as a space of "radical possibility" and as a "site of resistance" (hooks, 1990, p. 341).

Jerome Bruner, psychologist, says that we think in story form and that the most poignant and omnipresent symbolic activity is the story form. Writing about our lives doesn't just record events, it helps us define and develop ourselves as human beings and prepare us for the next transition. You hear the women doing just that—making meaning and making sense—as they write.

It's a literary collection, yes. These women wrote as strong as the "schooled writers" I teach at the University. But, it's also the writing of women who live in a homeless shelter, who may or may not show up for the voluntary class because of other responsibilities, who may or may not still live there the next week you show up, who may or may not want to trust you with the only story they have left— the story of becoming homeless. Note that I say "becoming" homeless. As you read this collection, you will learn it is a complex process.

The only place we could meet with the women was in the community room, which is also the dining hall. A dining hall that serves hundreds of meals a day; it's always noisy, and it's always hot. We had only two time options to meet with the women. After lunch or late in the evening. Homeless women at Wheeler are busy. They work at the Center or outside of the Center trying to get enough money to live outside, they take classes, they have programs that must be followed, they are filling out paperwork for employment, housing, disability. We opted to meet with them after lunch, hoping that if we came early, we could encourage the women to stay and have coffee and desert (not typically served at meal times) for our writing sessions.

But, we discovered that we didn't have to entice them with food at all. The women who participated, came because, like all writers, they felt an urgency, a need to purge their stories. They couldn't write fast and hard enough. They filled their pages, writing and sharing for 2 to 3 hours at each session, and then took their notebooks and wrote even more outside of class. It was a good challenge, but a challenge to keep up with all of the transcriptions.

Some of the women at Wheeler are recovering addicts, some have physical and mental health issues, some have suffered such horrific abuse and grief so deep that when you read it, you realize how insignificant your Netflix movie or your reality TV is. This reality "show" *is* real.

Wheeler accommodates 100 or more women at a time, and I had 20 show up to write, but only 15 consistently. And we lost several along the way. They couldn't handle living in such a confined space with so many other women or they struggled to abide by the rules or they couldn't stop using, so they

returned to the streets instead. We got to know the
women at these sessions and intimately while
transcribing and editing their stories. So, when each
week, we would learn that someone else left, it was
heartbreaking. One woman went out for a cigarette
and never returned. She left what she had there and
never came back. Another was more than half way
through the drug addiction recovery program and
found drugs, took them, and never came back. She
went home to the only home who gave her comfort,
Meth. We had other women who were there with
children who found placements elsewhere where they
could better care for their children. They didn't get to
finish their stories.

I wish I could characterize these women for you. But,
you will see their images and read their stories. They
are nurses, teachers, mothers, bakers, legal assistants,
athletes, animal activists, poets, chefs.... they are
smart and strong. Don't ever equate homelessness
with weakness. I've never met a more brilliant and
determined group of women. They've seen and lived
lives we can't fathom or imagine. Their stories will
read like nothing you have ever read before. As many
of them note, they shouldn't be here—they should be
dead. But, they aren't. They survived the end of
their stories, and they are still living to compose more.

One of the women, Diane, stopped abruptly one day
while writing a story about her divorce and heartache
and instead wrote about her favorite family pet.
Another woman was talking about how she missed her
pets, and Diane felt the need to talk about her beloved
pet as well. (This is what I love about writing in a
community. Someone else's story reminds you of your
own.)

"Having a family pet," she says to me, "is a luxury for
those who have means." And only once in her life did
she have that luxury. A woman who had lost babies, a
job and man she loved, caring for an adult son with a
mental illness wrote about her dog, a beloved rescue

Siberian husky. The dog was dying, had tumors all over her body, but the dog refused to show pain.

Diane wrote:
> These kinds of dogs do not show their pain, because they are a lot like the wolves in the wild. They like to run in packs together. If they show pain, the others attack them and kill them to put them out of their pain. Not to be mean, but to show their love of not wanting to see them or hear them in pain.

For me, these women, this summer in this special writing group, ran in that same pack. The women supported each other, listened and read each other's stories, swapped stories and ideas, and spoke in hushed and solemn tones about those who left and never returned. They never showed pain, only pride.

Where Mercy and Truth Meet comes from Psalm 85:10-11. I titled it so because Wheeler is a faith- based mission and all of the women identify as being Christian, and I wanted to honor their commitment to their faith. And when I began investigating verses, several notations talk about how this passage refers to those who are homeless, seeking reconciliation. It's really a perfect and beautiful verse to describe these women who are seeking peace and mercy, who by telling their truths, also seek righteousness.

hooks, b. (1990b). Marginality as site of resistance. In R. Ferguson, M. Gever, T. T. Minh-ha, & C. West, C. (Eds.), In *Out there: Marginalization and contemporary cultures* (pp. 341-344). New York: The New Museum of Contemporary Art.

Different Yet the Same
Tracy Line, Volunteer

It took but a matter of minutes for the walls to drop, the facades to fade and the stereotypes to be left at the door. I think it's because this time, we got right to the heart of the matter.

It is my third summer to volunteer with the Indiana Writers Center's Building a Rainbow program, but somehow this summer has stood out for me. As a writer, I love the program and everything it stands for; supporting others in getting words to paper, coaching them to explore their creative side, watching them find joy in what makes me tick (writing): it's wonderful.

But as a person, I love it even more. I love taking a step into another's world and learning his story. For me, I guess, it's all about bridging gaps and making connections with other souls, souls that might not otherwise have ever met.

In the past, I've worked with kids, but this year the program offered the opportunity to work with homeless women at Wheeler Mission. As soon as I learned of this, I felt drawn to volunteer here. I'd never worked with the homeless before and figured the program might benefit them in a multitude of ways. It may be selfish or completely arrogant, but I wanted to be a part of that.

The truth is, before this experience I knew next to nothing about homelessness. I've never been without a home, never known anyone who was homeless, and have never worked with the homeless.

Day one brought a touch of fear. My anxiety was not only due to the fact that I'd be driving out of my safe suburban neighborhood to an inner-city mission, but also (mostly) that I'd be face to face with women I presumed would be very different from me. I couldn't have been more wrong.

While our life circumstances and struggles aren't the same, our hearts indeed are. Each of these women has (as do I) hope for a brighter future, worry over past mistakes, and a desire to be loved and understood.

My heart about fell out of my body as the women read their stories. As I heard them read lines about their experiences-words describing abuse, addiction, and self-proclaimed failure, I understood the emotions behind them: fear, shame, denial and confusion over what it really means to love and be loved. Such sadness they've had to experience, mine cannot compare. Yet do we not all struggle, to some degree, with these very same emotions?

Class by class found me feeling bonded to the women. I began to understand their pain, celebrate the successes they were experiencing while here at the mission, and cheer them on for dreaming big about their futures. The words on paper and conversations about writing had created a sisterhood of sorts.

A few weeks in, I went to class to discover one of the women was gone: She'd relapsed and "lost her bed." There it was: my heart aching for a woman I hardly knew, but knew everything about. I may never know what happens to her. Only prayer lessens my sadness.

Many of the women (but not all) are overcoming addiction. Their stories reveal what drugs and addiction have done to destroy their lives. But one woman, Valerie, shared stories about the highs and lows of being an addict and drug dealer. When considering addiction, most of us envision a life completely out of control, a life where one is simply living for the next high. Valerie admits to that as well. But what Valerie showed me is that addiction doesn't start here. It left me to wonder: at what point does it come to that? (At what point does anything we ignore or deny lead us to a place where things fall apart?) What I learned from Valerie is that addiction is as sneaky as a slithering black snake.

Valerie's stories struck me: they are honest, colorful and humorous. Her life of highs and lows reveal to me her inner strength, intelligence but also her vulnerability. Addict is just one facet, one adjective among many, to describe her. And I realize: at our core, we women are all the same. We are all human. We are full of highs and lows, a complex combination of strength, weakness, intelligence, and vulnerability.

Addicts or not, homeless or not, we are all a mixed bag of adjectives. It takes learning to focus on our positives, believing in ourselves and in our abilities, to overcome. Overcome weakness, shame, guilt and the lies we've perceived from the world. The women of Wheeler Mission may just now be learning how to do that. But as they do, no matter where they've been, they can better themselves. Be something more. And I believe, with all my heart that Valerie, and the many women I've met in this class, will do just that. And I am cheering them on all the way.

Chandiss
Foster Care, Forgiveness, & Dreams

Foster Care, Forgiveness, & Dreams
Chandiss Harvey

I Remember...

I remember when I went to Walt Disney World for
my 10th birthday.
I remember when I lived in New York City.
I remember going on a Gator ride in Florida.
I remember making cheesecake for church brunches.
I remember getting raped.
I remember taking hot bubble baths.
I remember giving birth to my son.
I remember wetting the bed at night.
I remember losing my son.
I remember falling.
I remember getting my son back.

Scars

On Memorial Day 2014, I decided to take a walk to
my boyfriend's mom's house. It was very hot so he
met me halfway. I took his bike and road to his mom's
house. Once I got to her house, I put the bike on the
porch and went up the stairs. I knocked on the door,
and then the next thing I remember is waking up on
the bottom of fifteen stairs. I had blacked out from the
heat.

I had a hematoma on my right eye and scratches on
my left eye. Went to the ER to get an x-ray to make
sure I didn't break or bust anything. But that's how I
spent my Memorial Day 2014, and got the scar that
you see on my left eye.

Foster Care and Homelessness

Hello my name is Chandiss Chaneese Harvey. I was
born in Toledo, Ohio. I was raised in Sandusky, Ohio.
I really can't tell you much 'bout my childhood. When
I was in first grade, I went into foster care for the
whole year. By the time I was in second grade, my
grandmother got me out of foster care. She raised me

till I was 15 years old. I went with my mother at the age of fifteen, and I started failing high school. I dropped out at 9th grade.

At the age of 16, my mother gave up all parental rights to my sister. I didn't want to stay there with my sister no more. I gave myself up to Children's Services. I aged out of foster care at age 18. Ever since then, I been going through homelessness. I lived in Cleveland, Ohio since I was 19 up to the age of 24 years old.

Then, I moved to Indianapolis to just start fresh and over. And, now I'm at Wheeler Mission. My son is living with my grandmother. I'm working now, and I'm hoping to have my own place with my son and start over.

What if?

What if I wasn't born?
What if I was adopted?
What if I finished school?
What if I never had a son?
What if I didn't have my grandma?
What if I never smoked?
What if I wasn't in a shelter?
What if I couldn't see?
What if I didn't have feet?
What if I had a good job?

What have I lost?

Shoes
Clothes
Apartment
House
Job
Grandpa
Aunt
My Mind
My Son, but I got him back.

I Got Him Back

In the year 2013, I lost my son to Children's Services. I fell in a dark place. I was drinking, smoking, and popping pills. I only got to see my son once a week every other Thursday. Then a year goes by and then I got to get him dropped off at my house, spending overnights with me.

Then in the year 2014, December 3, the courts gave me my son back. So now I stay here at Wheeler Mission, while I try to get housing. I left my son with my Grandma, so I won't have to have him here in this place till' I get a place. But the Lord blessed me with getting him back, out of the system, and home with his birth mother. I thank the Lord for helping me to stop drinking and doing drugs. And focus on getting my love, my son back.

I Have Not Forgiven

I have not forgiven my mother for all the things I went through in my life growing up as a child.

I have not forgiven the belt hit that got me taken away from her as a first grader.

I have not forgiven the time she took up for her man raping me at the age of 10 years old and stayed with him for 10 more years.

I have not forgiven her for giving me up at the age of 16 years old.

I have not forgiven her for putting me and my son out on the street with no place to go.

I have not forgiven her for not being a mother to me my whole life and showing me how to be a respectable woman of this world.

I have not forgiven myself.

I have not forgiven.

Run Away

You and me gonna run away to
a quiet place where we can
make Love all day.
Boy, I know you feeling me
its so plain to see
this was meant for you and me
for you and me.

I Dream Of Love

I dream of a house.
I dream of a good paying job.
I dream of a million dollars.
I dream of space.
I dream of love.
I dream of happiness.
I dream of a car.
I dream of a good life.
I dream of being in the sky.

What Terrifies Me

I am terrified of losing my son again.
I am terrified of getting raped again.
I am terrified of not getting my education.
I am terrified of killers.
I am terrified of robbers.
I am terrified of being homeless again.

Chandiss, A Benevolent Queen
Barbara McLaughlin, Volunteer

Chandiss's subtle humor is a breath of fresh air in the overheated lunchroom where we meet to write. She doesn't work hard to be funny—she just is. When she reads aloud from her notebook, her delivery is dry with a dash of attitude. As she interacts with volunteers from the Indiana Writers Center, her eyebrows are expressive, but not in an eager or intimidating way. It's more of an *I'm on to you 'cause I've seen it all* furrow that gives her a weary credibility and a right to judge. Her mouth can let you know if she's pleased or annoyed without saying a word.

There's something regal about Chandiss as she strolls across the room and sits at one of the ten or so tables. She carries herself like a benevolent queen—gracing you with her presence as long as you don't take yourself too seriously. And when she whips off her black elastic headscarf, ruffles her color-processed hair, and makes it stand on end, you know she doesn't take herself too seriously either.

Her writing style is spare and matter-of-fact. There is power in her honesty. She gives equal time to the good and the horrific. She's a cooperative student, using a variety of writing prompts and methods to tell her stories. Each piece is captivating and illustrates the depth and complexity of her life, her loss, and her love.

When Chandiss gives me one of her looks, I smile spontaneously. I feel a motherly protectiveness toward her—though I know the word *mother* is a painful term for her, the opposite of protective. Thank God for Chandiss's grandmother who showed her how to love and perhaps gave her that subtle humor. I want so badly for Chandiss to keep her job, her son, and her place. And, I want her to know my affection and prayers for her are as genuine as my laughter.

Never Give Up
M.K.B.

I get my spirit from my mother. She never gave up on
me.

If you told me a year ago I would be here—here in a
shelter for homeless women— I'd say "you're lying."
But let's start at the beginning, rather then where I'm
at. Thirty-seven years ago, I came into this world. I
was 5 pounds and 5 ounces. I was two weeks early.
My grandpa Charles lost a fifty-dollar bet on me. He
thought I would be born the next day.

I was born with Cerebral Palsy. My beautiful mom
was only seventeen at the time. My mom took me
home and started physical therapy and helped me get
stronger. My mom chose to raise me. Therapy was
hard, but it was worth it. Every day I would stretch
my muscles, and my muscles were always sore. I
remember that I always thought my mom was the
best. She and I were more like sisters than mom and
daughter.

Between ages 1 and 3, my mom divorced her first
husband. I don't remember him. My mom noticed I
was behind in my walking around this time. She took
me to the doctors, and after running a lot of tests, an
older doctor tested me for Cerebral Palsy. I was found
to have suffered from a lack of oxygen at birth.

It was just me and my mom for seven years. My mom
had a few boyfriends. None were good to her or to me.
I remember a few times when Dave (I think that was
his name) threw my mom off a balcony and set fires to
everything we owned. I kicked him in the balls when I
was about six or so.

At seven, I became a big sister. I was so excited. My
mom brought home this little boy who everyone
adored. I wasn't allowed to hold him much because I
was young. I wish I could remember more about him.
But a month later he died. They said it was SIDS.

At that time my mom, understandably, went into a deep depression. I don't remember much about this time, just my mom crying and crying and crying—nonstop.

When I was 8, things changed. My mom fell in love with a trucker whose name was Mike. He dated my mom awhile and then left. Nine months later in May, my sister Angel was born. Let's just say that by age eight, I didn't have much faith in men.

Another place where I got my spirit from is Grandma. She was awesome. She never let me give up on anything. She encouraged me to make mistakes and learn from them.

Because my mom was only seventeen when she had me, I was closer to my grandma then my mom. Grandma Mary was funny and loved God. She played a major role in my life. It still hurts to think of her even though she been gone so long, over twenty years now. She loved to cook. I remember when I was four, and my grandma showed me how to pinch the piecrust on top. Her favorite dish is one of mine too. She called them German Strudels. Though I believe they're closer to a Pierogi. A meat filled strudel with onions and spices, which is steamed then baked. It was an all-day project. I haven't had them in a long time.

I used to talk about everything with Grandma. Nothing was off limits. My mom had issues talking about certain things that my Grandma didn't. I lost my Grandma at seventeen when she died of liver failure because of drinking, and had also contracted Hepatitis C from a blood transfusion. I was devastated when she died. I thought of killing myself just to be with her. Finally someone told me something. He said, "She loved you, and she didn't want you to follow her. It's not your time." I didn't understand it at the time. What he meant was God had a lot more for me to do and still does.

I remember the day my grandma passed. I remember the night before having a dream of her being in a coffin looking up at my family all crying, watching the tears fall. I realized I saw myself by a tree sobbing, hard. I woke up and told my mom. She told me to go to school. We would go see my grandma when I got home. A few hours later, my Aunt Pam came and got me at school and took me to the nursing home. Later that night, my mom told me to go downstairs in the nursing home and eat. I didn't want to, but did as I was told. I was praying as I felt her pass. I started crying as my cousin Marybeth came down crying. She told me my grandma was gone.

I have had more Bad things in my life then Good. But I have always loved God. I have always figured God must be preparing me for something better and great.

My son is that something great. I love him more then I have ever loved anyone. I know God don't make mistakes, that much I have learned. I will never give up on him or quit loving him.

I miss his smile. I love my son. I'm so proud of him. I didn't realize how much until I lost him to Child Protective Services. My son is 7. Already a lot like me, he has had challenges that we have both had to overcome. My son has a genetic disorder called Leukodystrophy and at age two was also diagnosed with autism.

Four years ago, I thought his Leukodystrophy was a death sentence. Most with this disease don't live past ages 12 or 13. But God blessed him, because so far he hasn't progressed. He is improving if anything.

The day I gave birth to this child was a cold rainy day in Los Angeles. It rained all day, but when DJ came out, the sun shone through the clouds and my husband dedicated him to God.

DJ from the time he arrived could evoke love from anyone who saw him. He as a baby would be on a bus and people would just give him all sorts of things. I remember once a woman told us God told her to give our son a crocheted blanket. We accepted it. DJ is doing work for God. I don't know what it is, but it's not for me to know but it's for God to know.

You should know that I wasn't always the way I am now. I was once a strong person, but people telling me what to think, always putting me down, eventually made me weak. I started to believe the Devil's lies. I took my anger out on my son and my husband. Child Protective Services got involved in my life about a year ago. It started with my son getting a sinus infection—his nose wouldn't stop running. So, someone turned us in. I couldn't believe it. CPS took my son, then my husband left—all within the same week.

After my husband left, I had to leave my apartment and went first to Queen of Peace, a temporary shelter. I was a wreck emotionally. I didn't eat or really sleep for close to three weeks. I called other shelters and got into the Wheeler on October 15. I believe God wanted me here.

Someone once asked where do I get my faith. My faith came about when I was a little child. My grandma and mom would pray for me and any others that needed it. I loved God because I should have died at birth according to the doctors. According to doctors, I should have never walked, talked, or gone to college. Because God blessed me, I'm a mom of an amazing little boy.

What I miss the most is the little things with DJ. I miss things like playing "happy" for the billionth time just to see him laugh. What I miss most is the quiet times with my son. I miss the way DJ looks at me and grins. I miss reading the Bible out loud to my child.

I'm writing this as inspiration to other mom's or dad's dealing with autism or Leukodystrophy. Your child is more then the diagnosis that they have. God has a purpose for special kids. I have to believe that. He had a special plan for me.

The doctors told my mom that I wouldn't be able to do a lot of things. All of which I have done and exceeded, because of God.

Before I Came to Wheeler and After

Before I did a lot of things I now regret.

Before I was nothing but a let down.

Before I had no value; I had no real talent.

After coming to Wheeler, I now know that God wants me. I have more self-confidence. I want to do new things. I see myself as God see me.

I have value.

I have worth

I have love.

Jessica
Strung Out on Misery Lane

Strung Out on Misery Lane
Jessica Shearer

I Remember...

I remember using drugs.
I remember not trying in school.
I remember being in jail.
I remember missing important events my daughter
had.
I remember my dad and mom fighting all the time.
I remember my daughter, Kylia's, dance recitals.
I remember having fun with Kylia.
I remember when I got diabetes and being so sick.
I remember the first time I smoked pot and injected
Heroin.
I remember my grandma's face when she died and
seeing her in my dream.
I remember my first wreck on my bike.
I remember the first time I had sex.
I remember several overdoses.
I remember wanting to die.

Bath Salts

The worst time in my life was when I used Bath Salts.
I was injecting them, so they didn't show on a drug
test. And I got hooked in such a weird way. I
absolutely couldn't stop. I quit my job of seven years. I
was crazy disgusting and wanted to die. I shot up all
day long. I was so paranoid. I wouldn't leave the
house. I stayed in my closet and picked at my skin for
days.

Bath Salts were an upper. I'd be up for days seeing and
thinking crazy stuff that I thought was real, but none
of it was. I weighed 140 pounds and was a disease. I
remember telling my mom that I repelled waters so I
showered all the time. I told mom I was afraid I'd hurt
my daughter so don't leave me alone with her. I have a
notebook I wrote in my handwriting, but I can't read
it. I would read the Bible to my friends and tell them

God is the answer, that he will save us. I'd write that we are killing ourselves. *We were.*

God was with me even at the worst times in my life. One time I went to the hospital. I thought in my mind that my mom had a party and had my daughter, Kylia. I thought someone stole all my needles, and I needed Insulin. So, when I went to the hospital I thought I was in danger. It was dark. They couldn't get an I.V. in to me, so they went in my neck. But I wasn't in any danger at all. I finally realized none of those things happened. So when I came to, to calm myself down, I had a friend bring me some Bath Salts, and I put it in my own I.V. at the hospital.

Before and After Drugs

Before using drugs, I played sports.
During sports, I started my first drug, pot.
Before pot, I was smoking cigarettes.
Before hanging out with my brother, I hung out with all my guys and my one best friend, Ashley, who was really smart. I didn't try.
After my best friend started hanging out with people who tried in school and didn't use drugs, I continued not trying in school, smoking pot and cigarettes.
Before, I didn't think I could get addicted.
After, I realized I did get addicted to everything that altered my mind.
Before, I was scared to do much or to be "messed up."
After, I thought I was untouchable and didn't care how much.
Before, I thought I could substitute one drug for another, rationalize my using.
Before, I said I'd never use the needle.
After, I fell in love with the needle.

Why?

As a child, my parents had their own problems, which affected me and my brother. That's where my false belief of being unloved stems from. I don't think I thought of it as being unloved until I got older and really looked back on it.

Why didn't my parents ever tell me that school is important?

Why was my mom so angry with us, yelling all the time?

Why was my dad acting like everything is okay?

They acted as if they didn't care about important things. They should have been teaching us.
Now I know they do love me, and they just had problems of their own. They needed help, and they never got it. It also goes back to the vicious cycle of generations. My parents weren't raised learning the importance of life. If they ever ask me for forgiveness, I will forgive as God has forgiven me for all the dirt I've done.

Soon I'll be asking my daughter, Kylie, for forgiveness about my past. I won't dwell in the past. I'll just try to make the future better, and with God I can.

Philippians chapter 4:13 says that I can do everything through him who gives me strength.

Dear Heroin

Dear Heroin,

When I first met you for the first time, I fell in love.
<3
I had the best high. Nobody gave me the high like you. We fought a lot. You left bruises and scars on my arms putting that needle to my vein of shame. I wore long sleeves to conceal you. I lost all my family and friends. I tried to leave. You turned your back on me, but you always got me back by that feeling you gave me. The bottoms where I'm at. Everything I ever had is gone, and another year's passing. After all you've done to me, I still love you and that needle. I'm

writing you to let you know you no longer control my life. I found a new love, and his name is Jesus, and he's faithful and will get me through everything.....
Goodbye forever and ever!

Former User, Jessica

Fear

Most of my life I have lived in fear of failing. That has set me back from doing a lot of things. I had accepted it, like it was okay to sit back and not try. Why start something if I'm not going to finish it?

Failure arises from selfishness, losing visions of goals, and not relying on God's strength, instead trying to rely on my own. The worst thing I can do is worry about the past failures, because it causes more failures. Failure is self-destruction.

Since being here I did many things I feared, such as talking or praying in front of people. I've done jobs that I was freaked out about, but being sober, being taught different ways to deal with things, and a lot about communication gave me some tools and has helped me.

If you catch me not doing something because I don't think I can do it.... fearing something, holding back, please ask me if there's something you could do to help me or just encourage me to do it.

Also, hold me accountable and most the time, if I'm told by someone who cares, I'll finish what I'm trying to not finish.

I WON'T let failure discourage me anymore.

How I Came to Live in a Homeless Shelter

My parents met young. My mom was 15, and my dad 18. They married when my mom turned 18, and my dad was about to go into the Army. They moved around a lot. They ended up in Hawaii. My mom was 21 and got pregnant with my brother Josh. Three years later, they got pregnant with me.

My dad was gone lots when my mom was pregnant with me, so they decided to move back to where their families were in Shelbyville, Indiana. I was born April 11, 1988. They got a house and that was the house I grew up in until about I was 16. My dad was an alcoholic.

Growing up, I don't ever remember my parents being happy. My memories start when I was about 6 years old. My parents got a divorce. My dad's family went to the courts and said things about my mom that was not true. I ended up having to live with my dad, which was not so great because I wanted to be with my mom. When I'd go to dad's from being with my mom, I would go crazy. I cry, throw fits, tear down curtains, and knock things over. I was hurting inside so bad. I felt like it was the end of the world.

My dad would party all night; I couldn't stand him. I remember looking at pictures of my mom and my grandma, and my dad said I wasn't allowed to look at those pictures anymore. My mom ended up getting custody of me. She got her own place, and she worked. My grandma took care of me. Pretty much, I had the same routine for about 13 years, which was church, staying with my grandparents on weekends, and the same thing before and after school, which was staying with my grandparents because my mom worked.

Looking back, Kylia, my daughter, is in the same generation cycle that I soon *will* stop. My brother was treated differently than me. He thought I was the golden child who got what she wanted and everyone's attention. I got things from mainly my grandma and then my mom would have to make it up to my brother. I've always felt like the only child. To this day, my brother resents me. It wasn't my fault. I've tried talking to him, but he just gets angry with me.

I loved sports: softball, basketball, AAU basketball, cheerleading, and volleyball. I stopped all that when I was about 15. I'd always wanted to hang out with my brother's friends. They were all into smoking pot. They'd go to the garage, smoke and hang out, and I'd be right there with them. My parents knew what they were doing. Looking back, my parents should not have let me go out there.

My mom was always mad at my dad because he was so laid-back. He'd go from job to job, and she would worry about bills, always arguing with him about them so that it made me worry. My dad being an alcoholic, my mom being so focused on her problems—they couldn't focus on us kids, so we pretty much did what we wanted and was never told the importance of life.

Failure started when I started smoking because my brother and all his friends smoked. My brother didn't want me to smoke so that made me want to even more. Eventually at age 12, his friend and I talked him into letting me. It made me paranoid, but I continued to smoke it every day after that. It made me laugh. Eventually if I didn't smoke, I didn't feel normal. I went from smoking pot to drinking to pills. I definitely got a feeling than that I didn't get with just smoking the pot. I liked the combination of it, because it made me not so shy. I could say and do things that I couldn't when I was sober.

During all this drug use, I hung out with all the guys and had one girlfriend. I loved getting the attention from the guys, but didn't want to be sexual. Most of the time, I didn't even want to have sex with them, but I just gave in and then felt like crap. Later in life, I realize they didn't want anything but to use me.

During high school, all I did was party at my dad's. My dad's house was the party house. There would always be at least ten kids there. Most of us dropped out of school. That lasted about a year until my dad's house got raided by the police. I just left and all the other kids ran out the back door. My dad ended up getting charged with everything.

That summer, I went into at least eight diabetic comas due to the drugs. My friends would have to call the ambulance each time. My dad was in the mix with all of us, and I had to take care of him and act like a parent of a child because he gets so messed up. I didn't care about school or try. I ended up quitting in eleventh grade and had no credits. I always worked. I started at McKay Manor when I was 14 until I was 17 and then went to Golden Corral for a year. That's when I really started using pills.

I played with different drugs such as Ecstasy and Crack cocaine. In 2006, I started working at Arby's. Then I got pregnant three months into working. I was only with my daughter's father one time. I stopped all drugs and had Kylia all natural.

I lived with my mom and six months later, I started snorting Heroin. My best friend, Burford, told me it was Oxys crushed up. Come to find out it was Heroin, so he ended up asking for my needles since I was a diabetic. I always had them. I said to myself, "What's another needle?" From the first shot, I was hooked. All my friends ended up shooting Heroin. We'd drive to Indy every day to get Heroin. Most of my friends ended up in to jail or dead. I ended up getting arrested for Heroin, a B felony.

After I got out of jail on bond, I relapsed and was arrested again for theft, then ended up relapsing on Heroin and Bath Salts, and then I went to a halfway house for seven months in Lafayette, got pregnant, relapsed on Heroin and Zainies, was going to have an abortion but ended up having a miscarriage. Failure.

I got arrested again for C and a D felony in August 2013, lost my job of seven years, went to jail, got out, and relapsed on Heroin and Meth. Failure.

Every relapse got worse, always Heroin mixed with something worse to make it more dangerous. I was in the hospital many times due to my diabetes and drug use. Nothing seemed to stop me. In all the years that I lost myself, I did drugs to numb my feelings. I was excused because I was a failure and did not have any responsibilities. During all the years of using, I always felt guilty. I *knew* I was not meant to live a life of self-destruction.

I knew I wasn't myself. I didn't want to be around my daughter, my family— I treated my boyfriend badly. After my last arrest and relapse, I remember lying in bed. I've been up for days on both Heroin and Meth, but I was so tired I couldn't move. Nana, my grandma, called me to let me know she knew what was going on, and she'd been praying about it. She said I needed to get help, and I didn't need to be around Kylia if I was going to continue. Coming from someone who is honest in her words, who loves me, made me make the choice to come to Wheeler Mission. That's all it took. I didn't want to let her down.

It was a relief actually. So here I am at the place God has put me to work on me. I have my ups and downs, but mainly ups. My worst crisis I had here was the beginning of Ms. Bethany's phase and poor Miss Francis was the one who got my word vomit but what encouraged me was Isaiah 30:20. I'd encourage you to read the footnotes because it's what got me out of my crisis. Although the Lord gives you bread of adversity and the water of affliction, your teachers will be hidden no more, with your eyes you will see them.

Formations

Life before Wheeler Mission was unmanageable. I didn't care about anyone or anything including myself. I did what I hated to do. No one, including myself, could figure out why I couldn't stop. At times I thought it would be easier if I would just die, a typical addict wanting the easy way out. I was selfish.

Deep down I was broken and overusing. I wanted something better for myself. I was ready to get clean and stay clean. I've been in rehabs, halfway houses, and jail. I would stay clean for a little bit, but always went back to what I knew; old friends, same town, no change, and resorted back to what I knew using. My Nana told me about Wheeler Mission, and I should go there. That was two years ago when I was shooting Bath Salts.

So, I finally made the choice to sign up for a fifteen-month program. And, I couldn't smoke? Wow, how was I going to manage that? But, I was ready for whatever. I used until the day I came here. I didn't have a worry in the world. I left everyone I loved and cared about, my boyfriend, my family, my daughter, and my friends.

Since being in this program, I have learned a lot. I am a beautiful child of God, and I am worthy. I am confident that I can increase my knowledge in all areas. God has taught me to live as he does. To treat people as he does. Not to worry, but to pray.

God has let me do my two favorite things here at Wheeler: laugh and smile. What a wonderful feeling to have joy and peace in my heart. A lot of my old negative and poor behavior leads to negative things. So I have realized how important it is to get rid of old habits and replace them with new positive habits. I have learned the importance of scripture and prayer; to turn to them when I need help, instead of my old behavior. Being sober, I've also found I can get frustrated and overreact. And Miss Frances would tell me, "Everything doesn't have to be a crisis."

I understand how big of an impact relationships can have on me and my recovery. I am beginning to learn from others mistakes, as well as my own. I'm learning to know the difference between a healthy and positive relationship versus a relationship in which I could get lost in or lose my focus. I recognize that some relationships can be a stumbling block for me, but I can learn from them and use the experiences to become more of an example.

Upon coming to Wheeler Mission, I believed in God and prayed. I went to church until I was 14. I even had my "ah-ha" moment in 2012 at Tara rehab. But, I still didn't have an actual relationship with God. I hadn't fully let him into my heart. I had never tried God's way. I really prayed about writing my story for this project.

But, God put it in my heart. He says, "Come to me when you are weak and weary. Rest snugly in my everlasting arms. I do not despise your weakness, my child. Actually, it draws me closer to you because it stirs up my compassion and my yearning to help. Accept yourself in your weariness, knowing that I understand how difficult your journey has been. Do not compare yourself with others who seem to skip along their life paths with ease. Their journeys have been different from yours, and I have gifted them with abundant energy. I have gifted you with fragility, providing opportunities for your spirit to blossom in my presence. Accept this gift as a sacred treasure, delicate, yet glowing with brilliant light. Rather than struggling to disguise or deny your weakness, allow me to bless you richly through it all."

Weak and weary?
Yes, I was.
Yearning to help me now?
Yes, and now I am yearning to have compassion and help others.
Has my journey been difficult?
Yes, I was gifted with fragility...easily broken.
When you begin being in my presence, do you blossom?
Yes, I do accept your gift. I do surrender, and I'm done struggling to disguise and deny my weaknesses. I now have allowed God to bless me richly through it all.

What If?

What if my diabetes had been taken care of at age
twelve?
What if when I was using, I stopped caring about
everything and stopped learning?
What if I had taken my blood sugars and not just
taken insulin here and there by guessing and only
because it felt high, being 500-600? Anything above
200 isn't good.
What if I hadn't missed that vein and ended up with
an abscess and a Staph infection?

Grandma and Grandpa

My grandma and grandpa Branson were my favorite.
God, I did some horrible things to them. I stole
money, jewelry, her pain pills, and Morphine patches.
She'd hardly ever take any of them so once I started, I
didn't stop until I was caught. But, I'd wait a little bit,
then start again. She really only said stuff about the
jewelry. I'd usually only take the pills to tide me over
till I could get Heroin.

I still was my grandma's favorite, till the day she died.
Me and my daughter Kylia were her favorite. She did
everything with Kylia as she did with me. We were
both spoiled by her. Her and Kylia used to listen to
the trains. Now where I'm at, I hear the train all the
time and I know it's her.

God, I miss her.

My favorite was sitting back watching Kylia and her
do the things me and her did, such as eating together,
playing out in her backyard, Kylia not listening and
running away from her giggling, her watching
whatever Kylia wanted to watch, and going through
old jewelry together.

God, I miss her.

Nightmares

I haven't been able to sleep lately, and I'm having all kinds of weird dreams. On the 15th, I dreamed I was trying to shoot up in the bathroom and Kylia was trying to get in. I was struggling to find a vein so I ended up throwing the needle in a bag and blood was everywhere.

I finally opened the door and didn't get to use. I never use in my dreams. The next night, I woke up crying. I had a dream that bugs were coming out of the rocks. I tried to kill them all at once, but they didn't die, and they were jumping at me.

Somehow in a dream, I ended up being at my grandma's, my favorite, my best grandma Branson.

I was with some boys and about to drink beer. I went in my old playroom where my grandma was sitting on a couch. I looked at her slumped over on the couch. I picked up her shoulders to where I could see her face, and it was my grandma's sick face. At one time my grandma was BEAUTIFUL, very well dressed, but once she got sick, she went down hill fast. I asked her what was wrong, and she said I wasn't allowed to go out on weekends.

That was the end of my dream.

As I woke up crying at 4 AM, I wished that Jon Boy could wrap his arms around me and comfort me. I had wished he was here to do that, but no one was here at Wheeler to comfort me. I lay in bed, crying, trying to fall back asleep.

Can't Sleep

I am thinking all through the night, and when I'm "sleeping," I still feel like it's not rest.

My mind races…

We are learning *in* here—at Wheeler—how to live *out* there—in the World.

Sometimes I have to ask myself what would I do out there? If I can't sleep, then I'll be tired. And, I will have work and classes and have to take care of Kylia. Whatever my responsibilities are, I need sleep or I will be worthless.

I prayed to God to help me relax my mind.

Don't be scared to ask for help.

Break the cycle. Do things different.

I don't want Kylia to do or think about anything without me. There's a lot of different things with me coming back to her in the cycle.

Give myself some grace. Factor in that my sugar might be low—deal with this.

Forgiveness

My goal is forgiveness.

Me and Jonathan Riley (Jon Boy) met in 2011. Him and his friend came to my house to get a needle because my friend Adrian told Joey and Jon Boy that I was "a cool chick who had needles," because I was diabetic.

So Joey called that night to ask. I told him, "If he gave me some." I was thinking he might give me Heroin, but it was just Bath Salts. So I was thinking, "I don't want that."

They called next morning, early. I crawled out of bed half asleep and met Joey and Jon Boy. Jon Boy says he told Joey, "I'm going to make her my girl." I sat in their car and Jon Boy had a knife that he used to give me the Bath Salts. They left to go work out. That was my first time meeting them both.

I had just gotten out of a relationship with Zachipoo. He was older, I think thirty-eight. I was twenty-three, I think. I had forgot to mention my healthy good relationship with Zachipoo. He was a great guy, a father figure. Kylia loved him. He went to school to be a nurse. Me and Kylia lived with him. Let's just say he had his shit together. He loved me and Kylia. But I relapsed once again. He tried to help. Paid for my counseling. I let my only healthy relationship go down the drain and hurt him and others in the process. I'd never had a healthy relationship. Failure.

Back to Jon Boy. Well he liked me, but me and Joey had something going on. Joey would get real jealous and say I was wanting to hook up with Jon Boy, and I wasn't. I was only with Joey. But, we all would hang out because were all on Bath Salts.

It was me and Joey doing crazy things. I remember one night in the Monster Green Truck, me, Jon Boy, Joey, Bath Salts, Zanies, and Heroin were all hanging out. We dropped Jon Boy off at his house. Joey and myself were really messed, nodding out. Joey was driving the truck with a a stick. OMG! I didn't know how to drive a stick. Here he was nodding out, and me trying my hardest to stay awake from the country through town to Adrian's, where we stayed.

That night Adrian locked me in the bathroom and shut off the lights. OMG, I was scared. He told me not to talk. Well, he ended up letting me out. I had no idea what he was going to do to me. Then Joey was mad, because I was in the bathroom with him. That's the weird jealousy part. I told him that I was scared he locked me in there with him.

Morning came. No sleep. Joey had slept a little. I woke him and told him I had to go home to be there with Kylia because my mom has to go to work. Anyways, he stands up naked and tells me I'm not walking. He's taking me home. He puts on his boots and a jacket. No pants—naked. He says, "I'm taking you home." I finally talked him out of it, so he went back to sleep. I put on his flannel shirt and ran all the way home in the rain. UGH! It was horrible.

I remember one time I had three hundred dollars. Me and Joey were going to get Bath Salts when I got off work. We stopped at Adrian's. We had both been up for days. We fell asleep, me laying on him. We had finally got some much needed sleep. Both had slept in bad positions, and we were stiff. Then it was time to refuel! More Bath Salts.

The weirdest time was when I went crazy and thought Joey was Jon Boy. Me and Joey went to get something to eat at Arby's. I ended up saying, "No, we can't." Freaking out so much we went to Burger King. We were arguing because he wanted me to eat more of the Apple dippers. That's when I started thinking he was Jon Boy, and I wanted to use his phone to call the cops on him. I was crying, wanting out of the truck. He told me no, so I kept on asking him to use his phone to call the cops on him.

He wanted to know what the hell was wrong. I settled down finally, but on the way back home I started grabbing the steering wheel. Jerking it. I did that the whole way home. I had done Heroin and Bath Salts that day and hadn't slept for days. I finally went to sleep. When I woke up, I was dizzy and fell backwards and smashed my trashcan. I called Joey. He came over, and I apologized after he told me what I did.

Now the best moment was when me and Joey went to the country in the middle of the night. We parked the truck and walked in an open field forever and ever. It was so nice out, and we just talked forever walking. The sky was perfect. Joey said he loved me all the time, and I told him the same.

We didn't love each other. Joey later would come into my life, and it was on once again. We went on where we left off. We were toxic. I do know Joey is like me.

He believes in God, and he is a good person. He has a good family who really believes in the Lord, but he fights that war against himself. That war against Addiction.

Joey ended up in jail. Then it was me and Jon Boy. We were always together for a long time. He slept with me in the same bed. He wanted a relationship, but I hated myself and only cared about myself and my Bath Salts. We never had sex. Jon Boy ended up in jail. He used to call me from jail, him paying for the calls. I was still doing Bath Salts. Then I ended up going to jail. He was in the block across from me.

I could see him and talk to him on the glass. I'd see him on the way to rec. YUMMY. I always thought he was cute, but while using, I didn't care. There he was with his shirt off. His build is oh so nice. He's 6'4, 210 pounds, and all muscle. I love everything about him: his eyes, arms, chest, and legs.

I was in love—instantly. So we started sliding notes under the door. One of his got caught, but one of the guards read it to me. We would three-way mail. I'd send it home, then they'd send it to me. One day I was waiting for court, and I saw the guard dragging his mat. The guard told me he left for rehab in Kentucky. I ended up going to a half way house in Lafayette. We would talk on the phone. I still didn't realize how serious he was. I mean I got pregnant by another man, UGH! Looking back I was horrible and selfish. He really loved me.

He ended up leaving the rehab and went back to jail and then to prison for a year. I finally relapsed and left pregnant once again in Shelbyville, Indiana and lost the baby. The sad thing is I didn't want the baby. I wasn't even taking care of Kylia. I didn't want anything to do with the guy who got me pregnant. So while Jon Boy was in prison, he was calling, writing, and once again I would answer the phone calls, but not really write. I was once again being selfish.

Joey came back into my life, and we were full force using. We stayed at my dad's in Indianapolis right where we got our Heroin. I remember something being wrong. He woke up, threw up, and couldn't walk earlier that night. I even had to help him shower. The next day, we got more dope. I went in the bathroom at the gas station and came out. Joey was blue. I thought he was dead. I gave him mouth to mouth. The windows were steamed up. I was crying, smacking him in the face. He was still blue. In my head, I was like "He's going to die on me. Do I call 911 or have someone help me? I'm going to go to jail if I call!" And when Joey wakes up, he'll be mad.

I replied to myself, "What the hell? That's horrible! You are being selfish! He could die!"

If you have ever talked to people who does Heroin, there is always a story of someone overdosing. This is just how it plays out. He ended up coming out of it. He grabbed me, hugging me, saying, "I'm sorry, I love you, Jessica."

I said to myself, "Never again." I was so sad, hurt, and scared. I can still picture his face blue and the feelings and thoughts I had. His mom wanted to help us both get treatment once again. I went to stay with my sister. He left. I think he ended up in treatment.

I went back to jail anyway. I wrecked my dad's car. Me and Jon were back to three-way mailing. When I'm sober, its love all over again, and I want my comfort, Jonathan Riley! This time, he got out of prison, and I was in jail; but we could talk on the phone. I remember saying, "I love you" for the first time to him. It didn't feel right, and he was caught off guard. I told him I was sorry, that it didn't feel right saying that and he agreed. The roles were switched. He was out, and I was locked up. I thought—payback.

Well one day, I wrote him saying something about how my friend Jason was going to bond me out. Soon enough, I got a card, a letter, and my favorite picture of him. My dad surprised me by bailing me out. Me and Jon Boy finally get to hang out sober. He'd come over to my dad's, and I remember his arms were so big. We watched the movie, *Bridesmaids*, and I laughed so hard. I love that movie.

After all those years, we finally had sex. We ended up texting and hanging out a lot. I remember lying in his bed and him telling me he does love me. He'd say he wanted to make sure I wasn't going to get close then hurt him like I always did in the past. Well we were good for a couple months. I was living with him and his parents pretty much. I started working at a Denny's in February. On Valentine's Day, Jon Boy surprised me at work with flowers, a card, and a new cell phone on his plan. I can remember coming out of the kitchen and him standing there. My heart melted.

But then, we both started using his Suboxone. I started using Suboxone and Heroin and then we were both doing Meth. It was toxic, and I turned into a total disaster. I was very mean to him. Jon Boy treated me like a princess, but the selfish using drug girl came out, and I'd say horrible things. He was so hurt, but he still didn't give up ever. To think about that makes me realize he really loves me.

I remember meeting Rich at Denny's, and he is now one of my best friends. Funny, he's gay and use to tell me how HOT Jon Boy is. Then eventually, we would all hang out. I ended up losing 50 pounds, and I was once again sick looking. I was doing a lot of Meth, and always Heroin when I was ready to come down. I worked all the time and I'd be up for days so my body hurt so bad that I'd have Jon Boy rub my back all the time. I remember on his dad's birthday, we did Zanies and Heroin, which is a lethal combination. He told me not to take anymore Zanies, but I thought I was fine. I couldn't keep my head from nodding. I don't remember his dad's birthday dinner at all.

When we got to his house, I shot up more Heroin. He wasn't in the room, but he found me on the floor and not responsive. He smacked me with his sandal. When I came out of it. I had ringing in my ears and could barely hear him. He took a picture of me to show me how bad I looked! I look at the picture now, and it blows my mind. Finally I slept. Meth had me spent.

What I Took For Granted

I've been in jail. I've used. I am at Wheeler mission.
I haven't been there for my own only child, Kylia.
My grandma was my rock, and now she's gone.
I hate that I couldn't be with my grandma while she was sick, because I was court ordered to be at Home with Hope in Lafayette, Indiana.
I can't raise my daughter how I want to raise her.
Being here now at Wheeler and clean, I want to reach out, to her help her, and be her mom, but it's hard being a mom from Wheeler. Really, I can't be her mom from here.
Using drugs did nothing but bad for me. You can't get anything out of using.
I took everything I ever had for granted. Every time I shot up, I was playing Russian roulette. Freedom …
Freedom is a wonderful thing—we just have to know how to act and what to do with our Freedom.
At Wheeler Mission, we can't have phones. We can't take walks for two months. We can't contact anyone for three months. We can only have visits here on the weekends.
Using drugs did nothing but bad for me. You can't get anything out of using.

After I had been in Wheeler for seven and a half months, I went back to Shelbyville. Only because I didn't have faith. My lawyer told me, "It's a year in prison or house arrest." I couldn't make it work at Wheeler at that time. So me and my wonderful case manager, Bethany, decided why spend the last two weeks at rehab?

Deep down my core was telling me to stay at Wheeler, but didn't have enough faith or trust in God that he had my back. So I ended up back in Shelbyville, not using and living with my wonderful boyfriend, Jon Boy, and spent time with my family, but was feeling "stuck" again. Same place. Same everything. Minus me and Jon Boy not using. What would change if I didn't change? NOTHING!

So the judge wanted to see if I could go back into Wheeler, but the phase I was in when I left Wheeler's Higher Ground addiction program was fifteen months, fives phases, so he set my court date back two weeks. I had that same judge for my other felony, and you know I could tell he felt I was really trying to better myself.

So I knew Wheeler wouldn't let me in the same phase, so I started working as a waitress and started taking G.E.D. classes. Still in my mind I thought, "Oh, I can do this." First day of work though, someone I knew asked for my needles. UGH! Looking back, I know God gave me that little bit of time in Shelbyville to grow me. I was "stuck" once again. I was sad to leave Kylia, Jon Boy, and my family once again. I ended up getting to go back to the Second Phase in the program. That meant going back to a group that had already formed.

When I was here the first time I learned so much, got really close to God, and actually had a relationship with him. He is the solution to staying clean. This time what has stuck out for me in staying clean is: God, Kylia, being a responsible adult, healthy relationships, and some type of support group. If I'm missing or not doing one of those, I need to reel it in. Get back on track.

Right now my plans are to finish this program and do what I have to for the courts. I want to continue working on my G.E.D., work on my relationship with God, find a job I like working with the elderly, kids or anything helping others, provide for myself and my family, for me, Jon Boy and for Kylia, and work on my relationship with all of them. I want to find a church and to have people around to encourage me. I want to find a hobby.

If I hadn't come to Wheeler Mission, I wouldn't have got the help I needed spiritually. I could have been dead, so thank you, Wheeler.

I hope my story helps others realize the war against our souls can be fought off if you roll with Jesus. Everything you read about was honest and horrible, but that's all behind me. I'm going to continue to work on my core from the inside out and keep going forward. Also, remember sometimes you fall, and you fail. Don't stay down. Get back up and keep moving towards the prize, Heaven. I encourage everyone to seek God because for me, He is the solution.

Editor's Note: Sadly, Jessica left the Higher Ground Addiction Recovery Program at Wheeler Mission in early August. We miss her contagious smile. Jessica contributed so many heartbreaking and hopeful stories to this collection. We pray that Jessica is continuing to fight to make her hopes and dreams become a reality.

Dear Guilt
Darolyn "Lyn" Jones, Editor

Jessica is one of the inspiring women I got to write with as part of this project at Wheeler.

Jessica wrote a Dear John letter to her "John"— Heroin.

> Dear Heroin,
>
> When I first met you for the first time, I fell in love. <3 I had the best high. Nobody gave me the high like you. We fought a lot. You left bruises and scars on my arms putting that needle to my vein of shame. I wore long sleeves to conceal you. I lost all my family and friends.
>
> I tried to leave. You turned your back on me, but you always got me back by that feeling you gave me. The bottoms where I'm at. Everything I ever had is gone and another year's passing.
>
> After all you've done to me, I still love you and that needle. I'm writing you to let you know you no longer control my life. I found a new love, and his name is Jesus, and he's faithful and will get me through everything….. Goodbye forever and ever!
>
> Signed, A Former User

I loved the writing style and tenor of her letter. This personification of Heroin as alive, as this person who loved her, comforted her, abused her, and controlled her. In our editing session, she shared how it was failure after failure that lead her to find comfort and solace and ultimately fall in love with Heroin. Every time she wrote a paragraph about a significant event in her life that lead her to Wheeler, she would add a one-word sentence. *Failure.* It became a refrain in her writing and in her talk.

Never feeling good enough brought her to a drug that *always* made her feel good. She reminded me of my own Heroin. My Heroin is my need to punish myself physically, spiritually, and emotionally for my son, Will's death and birth. I have had the same love/hate relationship with Guilt as she has had with Heroin. Guilt isn't my drug, but it's certainly a crutch that keeps me from standing up on my own and walking without it.

It's been 12 years since my son, Will's birth/death, and yet I still feel guilty. It doesn't matter what the doctors say, doesn't matter what the preachers say, doesn't matter what my husband says, doesn't matter what my friends say. *Failure.*

I failed to carry a baby, my only baby to term. I failed to get to the hospital in enough time to save him from a second brain injury. I failed to deliver him in time. Even after he survived, I failed to fix him. I failed to intervene with enough therapies or treatments or procedures to undo the damage. I failed to make him normal. I failed to spend enough of my time or money.

Now, rationally, I know this isn't true. His brain injuries were undetectable until they had already happened in utero. I spent more money than I had. I'm still paying those bills 12 years later. I spent more time than I had. Will had therapy every day for 1-2 hours a day and if I slept 4 hours in 24, it was a good night. I got him into the best specialists and programs and schools. But, it still feels like...*Failure.*

Jessica's drug use wasn't her fault. She was ignored; she was neglected; she was abused. She turned to the only family she had, Heroin. But she still sees herself as a ... *Failure.*

Hearing her and other women's stories of how they

have beaten themselves up and almost killed themselves for years of failures that were done to them (abusive parents, boyfriends, deaths, a screwed up social service and prison system) made me stop and take stock.

Jessica inspired me to face Guilt, to write Her a letter.

Dear Guilt,

I was introduced to you by my mother, who loved to live vicariously through you and invite or manipulate others to join the two of you in your daily Guilt fests. I grew up waiting for the bottom to fall out, because it usually did. And I would feel guilty about it even when it was never my fault. I was a child. Despite your tight grip and long finger nails that tried to claw me back, I was good at most things I tried: school, sports, creative projects. And, yet I was made to feel guilty for wanting more, guilty for trying.

Once I was cast as an outsider from my family, I ran into your maternal arms and held tight. You were the only emotion I knew. You helped me both cope and succeed. I would guilt myself into running faster, even if it meant injury after injury. I would guilt myself into staying up later and later to do more and more reading and writing so I could get into college someday. I would guilt myself into joining every activity and school leadership organization so I could be successful.

I had the best high when I was running faster than anyone else, hitting the ball harder and farther than anyone else, acing tests, and winning awards. Nobody gave me a high like you. You got me where I wanted. But, we fought a lot. The more I did, the more you wanted me to do. I thought you might ease up, but you never let up. It was exhausting.

Guilt, you forgot to remind me of your denotative definition, which is a feeling of remorse for an offense, a wrong, a crime. I had committed no wrong, but if I didn't do what you asked; I was responsible for not being good enough. I hid you behind a smile and an "everything is excellent" attitude, never revealing how sleep deprived, anxious, and sick of it I was. I alienated many of my family and friends. I tried to leave you. I came close. I was finally feeling settled with a loving husband and a successful career. But, then Will was born dead. The bottom's where you got me. I came running back to you for comfort.

Twelve years have now passed since you returned with a fierce stronghold on me. And, I have clung to you for help and support to once again cope and succeed. After all you've done to me, I still love that you helped me succeed, and I'm tempted to keep you around.

But, I'm writing to let you know that you no longer control my life. I have found a new emotion. I haven't failed. Will wasn't "done" to me. He *isn't* a failure. He's a gift, my joymaker. And I didn't fail him any less then he was failed by how he came to this World. He came to me as a part angel/part boy. Shit, I should be feeling like Superman's adoptive mom, Martha Kent. You no longer control me, Guilt. I am not a Failure.

Signed, A Former Mother Guilt Addict

Spiritually Sick
Anonymous

I have been spiritually sick for a long time. I often sit and wonder "What and why? Why do I have to have such a horrible disease? What did I do to deserve this? Why did I have to fall so far before I realized how sick I really was?"

I try to think back to when I was a child. Trying to pinpoint when my addictive behaviors started. I have not suffered from any traumatic events in my life. I'm always trying to find a good reason for why I'm this way.

But, if someone asked me to sum up my wild life in a few words or how I felt about myself, I would say a fat, unhappy person who is never comfortable in her own skin.

So what, you might ask, landed you in a homeless shelter, in a five-month recovery program for addicts? I guess what it boils down to is that I never learned to deal with my emotions.

As a young child I was always kind of chubby. I liked to eat a lot. I can remember getting made fun of occasionally. I wasn't exactly bullied, but kids will be kids, and I was devastated by it. At a very young age, I developed negative feelings about myself. I was an overweight child, and my father was very worried about me. He grew up as an overweight teenager and knew now that he just didn't want me to have to go through what fat kids go through.

My dad was always trying to bribe me to lose weight. He would say things like "if you lose 50 pounds, I'll give you $100 dollars."

It didn't work.

What if?

What if I was beautiful?

Would people like me more?

What would make me beautiful?

Is it the color of my hair?

Or the size of my breasts?

Is it the shape of my bottom?

Or the way I dress?

If I feel beautiful, would people

Think I am beautiful too?

If someone told me I was beautiful,

Would I really believe them?

Why is it that my whole mood can change,

Depending on how beautiful I feel?

How can something so meaningless as feeling being
beautiful or not,

Lead me down such a dark path?

Diane
The Dark Side & The Bright Side

The Dark Side & The Bright Side
Diane Fields

The Dark Side

I shouldn't be here.

This is how I felt when I first came to Wheeler
Mission. All I am doing is taking up space here on
Earth. Taking food from other people that need it
more than me. The only reason why I am still here is
because God does not want me yet. I don't know why.
I don't know what he wants me to do. I don't know
what path he wants me to go. I don't want to live like
this anymore. I am tired and worn out—physically
and mentally.

Diane is stupid. Diane does stupid things. I don't like
her. She doesn't learn. She keeps making the same
mistakes over and over again financially. I am tired of
fighting with her over and over about finances.
Robbing Peter to pay Paul. Just barely making it
work. Sliding by just to survive.

I don't believe I was put here for that kind of life. I
just want to be by myself in a house with my cat. The
way it used to be. I want to plant flowers and have a
garden. If I can't have this kind of life, then there is no
reason for me to be here any longer. I don't want to
live here if I cannot live my life the way it should be. I
feel numb, don't care about much of anything
anymore. Don't care if I am here or not. Just go with
the flow for that moment and time and in that
moment and time. Just trying to get through the day
the best I can for the moment. I feel like I am living in
limbo. Not knowing is the hardest part.

Don't know where to go from here. If anywhere. I just
feel like I can't get through one more moment in my
life. Just can't make one more decision. Can't make a
decision that is right. Always making the wrong
decision. Just don't do anything for fear of doing the
wrong thing or making the wrong decision. It's like

the dark side trying to come out. Crawling out of a dark hole. I feel like a failure to myself and my children. All I wanted is and was to have a permanent home. A stable home for my family. Is that too much to ask for? But I messed that up. Not only once, but two and three times. Maybe the timing wasn't right. I hate myself for it.

Scared of Heights

I ended up at the homeless shelter because of losing my job.

My son got an apartment. I helped him with the payment and furniture he rented and his truck, to give him a head start. Then he lost his job and everything. He moved into my apartment and stayed for a while looking for a job. Then about two weeks later, I lost my job after being there for seven years. They laid me off, gave me a severance pay, and said my job was eliminated. I went on unemployment for six months, and I used part of the severance pay to live off of. I could not find another job for six months. Never did find a job. I have some physical and emotional problems. It was hard to find a job. My son stayed with me for a year at a room that you rent. It was rough.

The financial place repossessed my car, so we had no way to get around but walk. Neither one of us had ever rode a bus before. Didn't know much about it. How much it cost or about the bus passes either. We only had about ten or fifteen dollars left after paying for the room. We ate peanut butter and jelly sandwiches for weeks and drank water. Then we found out we could walk to the church and get food, health, and beauty supplies. We did this for about a year until my unemployment ran out. I eventually lost my apartment and my car and everything except my furniture because it was paid for. My furniture is at my daughter's house, but because of certain circumstances I am not allowed to stay with them at my daughter's house.

Staying at the In-Law's

My son and I had to spend the night on the side of my daughter's driveway by the garage, because it was the safest place for us. In her neighborhood, there are a lot of police that live in her neighborhood. Her father-in-law would not let us, my son and I, stay at the house any longer. We stayed there for a week. He did not know we were there at first. My daughter's father-in-law owns the house. It was inherited and passed down to my son-in-law's mother.

My son has mental health issues and had paranoia real bad. Sometimes he didn't know how to do simple things that we take for granted like turning on a stove. Once, he started to make breakfast and didn't know how to turn on the stove. He panicked and just walked away because he didn't know what to do next. He says he didn't know what he is supposed to do. I told him to sit down and watch T.V. and that I would finish fixing breakfast. He also backed up in fear when my daughter lit up a cigarette to smoke. He backed up and asked, "Why is she doing that?" My daughter ran to the bathroom and put out the cigarette. You see my son used to smoke, but after the paranoia came he said he did not smoke. This all happened during the week we were staying there at my daughter's house. Because of this incident and the in-laws, we were not allowed to stay there.

I prayed to God and Jesus to guide my son and me in his direction. Where he guided us was to the church we both use to go to. Thank God for them being here. God is good all the time; All the time God is good! God is my sunshine! My daughter took us there in her truck and dropped us off at the church. The church called and got us a place at the Women's Wheeler Mission for me and a place for my son at the Men's Wheeler Mission.

Panic Attack

When I first arrived at Wheeler, Miss Liz, the counselor, said there was no beds available. I said the church people called here, and they said there was. I was so upset that I went back out, but the van had already left with my son. I didn't know what to do. I came back in and told Miss Liz that my son and the van already left. They had one bed left. I was scared. Something like this has never happened to me before. I was a mess, ready to have a nervous breakdown. I couldn't comprehend or understand why this had to happen to me. Miss Liz finally said okay, and she told me I could have the bed, but it was on the top bunk on the second floor.

I am afraid of heights. I had a panic attack. I could not figure out how to get back down. I was also claustrophobic. Too close to the ceiling. Too small of space. Could not breathe. When I got up there, I panicked and could not get back down. The girls helped me get down. The girls said for me to sleep on the couch and the nighttime guard said it was okay. I cried for three days. I was so upset. The next two nights, I slept in the gym. Then by a miracle from God, a bottom bed came open on the second floor. I stayed there for three months when a bed came open on the fifth, which is the floor for people trying to get on disability. The girls and Miss Liz were wonderful to me. This is the exact place I needed to be at that time of my life.

I was so depressed. If it was not for God leading me to the church and getting the help I needed, I would not be here today to share my story. Because I was so depressed and I didn't know what to do, I tried to kill myself, but God spoke to me and sent me to the church and then to Wheeler Mission. Thank God for the Women's Wheeler Mission. I thank God for his guidance and Wheeler Mission for saving my life. Thank you Lord.

My life has changed dramatically within this past year. It will be a year on June 23rd. I am so grateful for the Women's Wheeler Mission. Now I am waiting for my apartment and looking forward to living a normal life again with God in my life. To live a fulfilled and happy life. A long and prosperous life. Enjoying every beautiful day to the fullest. Stopping each day and smelling the beautiful flowers and the beautiful scenery that God has provided for us to enjoy and be happy. This hope puts a smile on my face everyday. I'm looking forward to the next day and the future. I'm even enjoying every moment of the present day and time that I am in right now.

Thank you Lord for this Gift of life.

Married Life

To me the happiest spot in the house I lived in from birth to adulthood was where my fiancé asked me to marry him. He got down on his knee and proposed to me while I was sitting on my parent's sofa in the living room. He put the engagement ring on my finger. Then he left and said to not say anything to my parents; he wanted to surprise them.

We had been dating for about a year before that. We had met through my girlfriend at the time. She knew a man that my fiancé knew. She saw him and asked them both to come over to the car. We were in my friend's car waiting for her boyfriend's boss to leave so she could go and talk to him. He was at work. This was in the evening. I told my friend that he looked cute. We got to know one another, and I moved in with him. This is when he asked me if he could kiss me. I had never been kissed like the way he kisses. It was great—very passionate, gentle. I fell in love right off the bat. So handsome and strong shouldered. Large muscles in his arms, cute little smile, and a kiss that swept me off my feet.

He came over to my parents' house that night, and he proposed and asked them for my hand. At first my parents were surprised. Then they asked are you sure that this is what you want. We both looked at each other and responded at the same time, "Yes." Then they said okay. But for some reason I got the feeling they weren't too happy about it. I don't think they liked him very well. After he left, they asked me if I was sure this is what I wanted to do. They felt he was too old for me. He was eight years older than me. But that did not matter to me. I was in love with him. So it felt like my mom was doing everything she could to try to break us up.

She took me to pick out a wedding dress. She said it would have to be an off white dress like a cream color, not a white dress, because I lived with him for a few months. If I wanted to have a traditional wedding, then I would have to move back into their house and get married in an off white dress. So I did. Then my mom wanted to get a two-tier cake instead of a three-tier cake because there was not going to be that many people there. That upset me because I wanted it to be a traditional wedding. So we ended up getting the two-tiered cake. She said we could put the top tier in the freezer for our first anniversary. I said okay, even though it upset me. It seemed like it was her wedding instead of mine.

Then we picked out the invitations and the girl there said yes, they could put greenery and blue flowers on the outside of the card and blue printing on the inside. They came out wrong with green writing on it instead of blue writing. So my mom sent them back and asked for different ones. It was just one hassle after another. So we decided to just elope because it was as if it was my mother's wedding instead of mine. She wanted everything her way, all the way down to colors even and the style of shoes too. So we ended up eloping at a church with a justice of the peace. His mother even had a bet with her son, my fiancé, that he would not end up marrying me. Can you believe she bet twenty dollars on us not getting married?

After we got married, his parents were there and in the parking lot his mother handed him the twenty dollars, and she said to him, "Don't spend it all at one place." We all laughed. He said he was going to use it to take me out to dinner. We all laughed again. I was just happy to be married. And we left to go on our honeymoon. We did go out to eat to our favorite place, a Chinese restaurant.

The Kids

So after we eloped, we began our lives and lived our lives the way we wanted. I ended up getting pregnant at the beginning of our marriage. It was a boy. He ended up being stillborn. I was in my first week of my ninth month. He weighed seven pounds and two ounces. My biggest baby. We buried him at East Washington Cemetery.

Thank God I could have more children though. Two years later, I had another boy. It was a perfect pregnancy. No problems at all. While I was pregnant for my third time, I did not know I was pregnant with twins. I miscarried with one of them. It was too early to tell if it was a boy or girl. We did not know if they would have been identical twins either. I am thankful that I did not lose both of them. My son is the middle child. Sometimes I wonder if the loss of his twin affects him or not. Like a loss of his life after spending time together and growing together even though it was a short time. I guess that is something we will never know. Only God knows.

Then two years later, I had another boy. It was a pretty rough pregnancy. I had toxemia built up, what they call preeclampsia, and he was premature. He was nine weeks early. He weighed four pounds and nine ounces.

Two years later, I had a little girl. She was premature too. She was eleven weeks early. I had her in my first week of the sixth month. She weighed one pound and fifteen ounces. She was like ten inches long. She could fit in her father's hand from head to toe, from the ends of his fingers to his wrist.

We had to get premature clothing for her, and they were still too big. So my mother and I went to the store and garage sales and bought doll clothes for her. Even the premature diapers were too big. We had to turn them down at the top. She was in the incubator for three months before we could bring her home. She had to get to over four pounds to bring her home. That was the longest three months of my life. It was very hard to leave her there at the hospital. But in my heart, I knew that is where she needed to be at the time. We would go up to the hospital to see her twice a week and bring my breast milk to her. I would sit and read this lion book to her. I could tell she liked it, especially when I would make the roar sound like a lion. She would smile. We put a picture of our family on her incubator so she could see us everyday.

She had a breathing problem where she would forget to breathe. A breathing apparatus had a beeper/buzzer that would go off when she would stop breathing, and the nurse would shake her bed and she would take a deep breath because it would startle her. Most premature babies are born like that. When we brought her home, she did that one time. It just happened to be when the nurse came to our home to check on how she was doing and how things were going. When we went into her room, she was barely breathing and her lips were blue. I gave her mouth-to-mouth resuscitation, and she was okay. The color came back into her lips. The nurse said we definitely needed one of those monitors, so she went out to her car and hooked it up.

I had to give her mouth-to-mouth resuscitation again one more time when she was taking her bottle. She vomited and was choking and it was coming through her nose and her lips started turning blue. It was like she couldn't get any air. Like she was still clogged up in her airway. So I gave her mouth-to-mouth resuscitation. She let out a cry. She was still kind of bluish looking though. So I called the doctor's office, and he said to take her to the emergency room just to be on the safe side. So we did. She was okay.

This is definitely my miracle baby. With everything she has been through, she is a very strong and strong-minded and willed girl. A very stubborn girl too. She was meant to be here. I love her very much. I love all my children. By the grace of God, I was allowed to have them. The joys of my life. They light up every day of my life, like the sunshine shining down on me and putting a smile on my face. Like Jesus putting his warm and loving arms around me. Thank you Lord for the gift of life, the gift of my children.

Divorce

It was one of the worst days of my life. I don't think I have ever felt so much pain and hurt in my heart by anyone in my entire life. You see it started when my husband didn't want me to have our daughter. She was the third child that lived. He did not want to have three children he said. He only wanted two children. He wanted me to have an abortion. I said I could not have an abortion with this child any more than I could have had with the two boys. He said what if it is a boy instead of a girl. I said, "Well, we will have three boys then." He was upset. That upset me that he even suggested a thing like that. I thought, *Who is this man I married?* But then as time went on and by the time our little girl was born he got used to the idea of having three children. At first he was okay with the idea. Then after she got about two years old, he started being mean. I don't want to go into the details here, but he was lucky he didn't go to jail.

After the divorce, he paid child support for a while. Then disappeared with the so-called "live-in" babysitter. He gave me a false address. It was a fire station address. We could not find him for over five years. Then my daughter said she found him. She found him through Google on the Internet. He left when our daughter was five years old. Now she is twenty-six, almost twenty-seven years old. He visited by court order and paid child support for one year after she found him. Then he stopped.

He came to terms with our oldest son. But the younger siblings, he did not want to have anything to do with them. They were of age by then. They had the right to see him or not. The middle son was hurt too much in his heart to forgive him. Some day, maybe he can come to terms with him in his own heart to forgive and let go. Maybe someday Jesus will be able to come into his heart and help him.

My ex-husband died of cancer. I held a grudge against him for what he did to our children and myself for so long. I had a lot of anger against him for a long time. Then after I came here to Wheeler Mission, I started going to church and found God and Jesus. One day I walked out of church, and it felt like cement blocks lifted off my shoulders and I forgave my ex-husband. It felt like I started a new life like being born over again with a fresh start in life. I feel like I have a new life to live. May God have mercy on my ex-husband's soul and forgive him and bless him.

My Son

My son went through a lot too. My son and his girlfriend had been together for five years. Then things did not work out between them and they broke up. My son was so hurt. He took a friend's medicine, which created paranoia for him. The medicine messed up his mind. He realizes now he should have not done that. Plus he got drunk along with taking drugs. He could not handle living at the Men's Wheeler Mission. He did not know what he was supposed to do. So he left and was on the street again. He ended up at Midtown Facility downtown because he had paranoia so bad.

He stayed there for about three weeks and before that he stayed at Methodist for about two weeks. Then after he stayed at Midtown, they sent him to Saint Pats where he stayed for about a couple of months,

and they helped him put him on the right kind of
medicine. The paranoia cleared up some. He went
through about two or three jobs. He could not keep
them because his paranoia was so bad. He would be
working, then the paranoia would come over him and
he would be like a 5-year old child who didn't know
what he was supposed to do next. So he would leave
and go home.

When we were staying for the one week at my
daughter's house, which was when my son had
paranoia real bad, he got up in the middle of the night
and went in my grandson's room and started putting
his toys, his cars, and trucks away in his closet, acting
like when he was a child. He said he had to put them
up so he would not get into trouble. So I had to tell
him to go lay down before he woke my grandson up.

After Saint Pats helped him as much as they could, he
ended up at the Men's Wheeler Mission again. He was
there for a while then met a friend he knew and he and
his friend got an apartment. The apartment is in his
friend's name but it is a two bedroom, so they became
roommates. My son got a job. Then lost it. He is in
the process of searching for a new job.

He met a friend he's known for twelve years. She has a
child. My son and the girl he has known since
childhood have decided to try and become more than
friends. They are dating. Praise the Lord. I think he is
going in the right direction now. He is going in God's
path. The Lord is guiding him and blessing him in a
wonderful and bright future.

Markings Like a Wolf

She was a Siberian Husky. Full-blooded. My children
and I, shortly after the divorce, went to the Marion
County Animal Shelter, and we picked out this dog.
She was beautiful. She had real pretty blue eyes. My
oldest son named her Ice because her eyes looked like
ice cubes with the sparkle of blue shining off an ice
cube. She was black and cream with a little bit of silver

look to her hair. Her markings I think made her look like a wolf. But she was very gentle. Even the kitten liked her. The kitten would lie on her back while they slept.

She was brought in as a stray. She was two years old at the time. She was already trained to sit and shake her paw. The kids taught her to shake with the other paw. She would run and get the ball and bring it back. She loved to play tug-a-war with her rope. She loved to chew on a rawhide bone. One Christmas I bought a great big, huge bone with big knots on the ends of it. It looked funny when she would play with it and carry it in her mouth.

But she got old. She was about ten years old when I had no choice but to have her put down. She had tumors in her body. One big one on her right elbow in the front leg. It got so big it burst and blood flowed out really bad. Her stool turned black looking. She was having a hard time going to the bathroom. Her urine started leaking really bad. The veterinarian gave me pain pills for her, but that lasted only for a few days. She was having a hard time trying to walk. Her back legs and hips were stiff like she had arthritis bad. I took her to the vet's office, and he said it was time.

These kinds of dogs do not show their pain, because they are a lot like the wolves in the wild. They like to run in packs together. If they show pain, the others attack them and kill them to put them out of their pain. Not to be mean, but to show their love of not wanting to see them or hear them in pain. So this was very hard for me. She was one of the family because we had her with us for so long. Every place we moved to and lived, she was with us. But I knew this is what had to be done. I had her cremated. We have her ashes in her own urn. So she is always with us, in our hearts.

Wheeler Woman

This is how the Wheeler woman's mission helped me through the year and helped me get back on my feet to have a wonderful and beautiful future. This is where I learned about God and Jesus the most. I learned I was not the only person in the world that had problems.

The women here are very helpful to me and understanding. The caseworkers are exceptionally good with people. They seem to know what to say at the right time. They are very compassionate and stern too when they need to be. They help with almost every thing from giving you the information you need to putting the right people in front of you to help you get what you need to get done. They help you with every aspect of your life. From giving you a place to live and food to the everyday toiletries we use to keep clean and decent. They help with how to get a job and to keep a job; they educate and help is with health and finances. They are educating us for everyday survival. They help you with everything to get a fresh start with life—a second chance to get your life back on track. Walk with Jesus, and you can't go wrong. With Jesus in your life, it's like the sunshine that puts the smile on your face for eternity.

What is the most powerful place to me?

Right here. Right where I am at—The Woman's Wheeler Mission.

This mission is the most powerful place I have ever been because the people here are the people that God put in front of me to help me through one of the worst trials and tribulations of my life. God is the one that guided me to this place. I needed the help and guidance from God and the people here. I didn't understand why and how this could happen to me. I thought what could I have done so bad that I ended up in a homeless shelter. I thought I did something so wrong that I was being punished for it. That's the way I felt when I first came here.

Little did I know that this is where God wanted me. I learned about Jesus and God. I learned why God brought me here, and why he kept me here for so long. I had a lot to learn about Jesus and God. I learned a lot about myself too. He, God, does not want to send me out into the population until he knows I am ready. I have been very patient, but I think I am very close to being ready. I feel I am ready to be back into the public as a permanent resident. To face the world with a big smile and enjoy what God has given us, mostly freedom.

The Bright Side

How do I see myself?

The peacemaker. Happy enjoying life. Enjoying crocheting. Sitting outside listening to the birds, and the peace and quiet. Looking at flowers and smelling them. Loving the sunshine. Wanting to be around happy and smiling people. Taking day to day. Being carefree everyday. Getting through the day the best I can.

If I am here at the end of the day or tomorrow, so be it. If not, well, I did the best I could. I tried. I am ready to go whenever God decides for me to. I just want to live the rest of my life the best I can, in a house with a cat that I can call my own. I want to cut the grass and plant some flowers and have a small garden. I want to just stay at home and enjoy my retirement until I die. I want to enjoy when my kids and grandkids come over and bake cookies together and visit and watch them play.

That's what I hope for.

Diane: Faith, Family, & Love
Jessica Mayo, Volunteer

If I had to use a few words to sum up Diane's writing, they would be faith, family and love.

Diane shared a range of experiences that were unique to her and universal to women at the same time. It was easy to connect with her straightforward style as she put to paper stories about the highest and lowest points of her life. In reflection, the purity of her words became clear, as they were unclouded with excessive descriptions or ego. It was the simple and honest truth, in the world according to Diane.

Diane's perspective on homelessness shocked me when she described it as a blessing. How could homelessness possibly be a blessing? It was something that I desperately feared, and worked and saved to avoid. Growing up, my family was not just considered low income, we were downright poor. Life on the edge as a child left me with a lingering sense of insecurity as an adult towards financial stability and difficulty in understanding this positive approach.

Of course, I should add that this was not Diane's original sentiment towards her lack of permanent housing. She felt the expected fear and desperation and even shared with the rest of the group that she was unsure if she wanted to live when she found herself at Wheeler. The other women nodded their heads in supportive agreement as she read from her journal about this time of her life.

When Diane finished, one woman chimed in, "That's how we all felt at first."

The woman said that for the benefit of the volunteers; the women of Wheeler already knew exactly what Diane was describing. They shared a bond over more than just a common, temporary address. Each of the women had survived deep loss and tragedy, overcome the toughest of life's challenges, and still managed to love, laugh and help others along the way.

Through the support of the staff at Wheeler and other residents, Diane came to see her world with a fresh view. She gained an appreciation for the struggles that she endured in order to find her voice and faith. Her stories show that life, while not always easy or fair, is a gift to be treasured in which she is grateful for the present and hopeful for the future.

Sara
Men

Men
Sara Casteel

I Remember...

- Going to the doctor for meds at a young age and taking meds before I could even swallow pills.
- Easter egg hunts.
- My dad hitting me till I was black and blue.
- Being told there was something "wrong" or different about me, and that I needed medication.
- Deciding to be like my brother and the "cool kids" and wanting to get hooked on cigs in 8ᵗʰ grade.
- Getting my first Morphine from two boys in 8ᵗʰ grade and getting expelled for it because my friend told on me.
- My brother's first friend overdosing and dying when we were so very young.
- Breaking so many bones while growing up.
- Watching my aunt pour vodka in her G-tube so she could get drunk and not taste it.
- Riding a horse for the first time.
- Splitting logs for the fireplace.
- Having crazy big parties, like every weekend.
- Almost getting arrested numerous times.
- My stepdad committing suicide.
- Smelling pot for the first time and finding out that my dad smokes it.

Introduction

Hi, my name is Sara Casteel, and I am going to take you on a journey through bits and pieces of my life.

As you read this, please keep in mind I am not a writer, so bare with me through this journey. Also remember there is so much more to my life than the memories that I have written in here. So many things that have happened that I just don't remember or didn't stand out or for whatever reason, God didn't put on my heart to share.

I am not looking for pity or sympathy because everything I went through in my life has made me the strong and God-fearing woman I am today. Also know that no matter what you are going through, there is always light at the end of the tunnel. I am proof that there is always hope of living life to its fullest without regrets even if there were so many times that you didn't know or care if you are were going to wake up the next day.

Men

I remember being abused by so many different men in many different ways. My dad was physically and emotionally abusive. I remember sitting at the dinner table and my sister was a little overweight, and my dad turning to her and saying, "No man will ever love a fat woman." He would tell her that she didn't have to finish her dinner because she was too big, and my brother and I were to sit at the table until all our food was gone no matter how long it took.

I loved my dad, but I didn't like him very much while I was growing up. I really barely knew him. He was always in bed or at work or administering punishment. There was this one day… I must have been in 4th or 5th grade, and I was mouthing off to my mom. She finally had enough and woke my dad to punish me. He was in a huge rage. I remember scrambling all over the bed trying to get away from him, and he just kept coming after me and hitting me over and over again with the paddle. I was black and blue up and down my back to the back of my knees.

My mom just stood over me crying saying how sorry she was after it was over. She was so upset at how badly I was bruised. I went to school the next day, and the nurse saw what happened. I'm not sure if anything ever came of it, but I know it didn't go unnoticed. My dad and mom divorced when I was about 16, and I introduced my mom to a man named Ray. By then I was drinking, smoking, and using drugs almost every day. My mom had started drinking daily during her divorce. Ray was a recovering alcoholic and started drinking again with my mom.

When he was sober, Ray was a great man. But when he drank, he became someone else completely. I used to have to drive him to the liquor store because he was too drunk to drive. There was this one time when I was 16 or 17, driving back in his Mercedes. He was drunk as hell and decided I needed to go faster. He put his foot on mine on the gas and floored it to 120 mph. It took all I had to not freak out and wreck. Thank God we made it back safe.

I finally started sleeping at friend's houses every chance I could because he would get drunk and think I was my mom and come onto me. Eventually I moved out and went to college and to the Army. When I got back from the Army, he was in legal trouble and swore he wouldn't go back to prison. He ended up leading the police on a seven-mile chase (drunk) and committed suicide by running into a tree at 70 mph. It was so hard on my mom. I held her for days before I could rest for a while myself.

I have since been in many abusive relationships with men. I have been beaten, raped, called names, and believed I wasn't worth anything more because I was an addict and an alcoholic. But the most abusive relationship I've been in has probably been the one with myself.

I have learned throughout my life to be the caretaker. When I was very badly addicted, I was still taking care of others. My grandma was dying of cancer and my mom, brother, cousin, and I all were staying there taking care of her. But we were all addicts at the time. It was always a struggle over who would get some of the pain meds she had. My cousin taught me how to break into the lock box that my mom kept the meds in. She eventually gave up and started giving me some every day so I wouldn't take them. My grandma never went without, but neither did we. It was so hard to watch her go slowly. She developed Dementia and kept saying she wanted to go home.

In December, she was bedridden, and I was very depressed. I woke up to sounds of her gasping for breath. I went straight to her room and found my mom silently crying holding her hand. I walked to the other side of the bed and my first instinct was to do CPR. But I knew it was time. She passed away holding my mother's and my hands. She was a huge role model to me, and I was named after her—Sara Rose. Her name was Rosemary (the most amazing and loving women I have ever known.)

When I was in high school, I took Early Childhood education because I always felt I could relate with those children who were outcasts and misunderstood. I also worked at a daycare ministry when I was 18. In vocational in high school, we ran a pre school. I loved working with the kids, making lesson plans and talking with them about their home lives. I had a volunteer named Debbie who was in a wheelchair who would come in and help the kids plant seeds in a cup. I worked with Debbie to teach the kids to not be afraid of wheelchairs, but to treat Debbie like a human being.

This was a time when I was very addicted to any kind of mind-altering substance, even though I wasn't aware that I was addicted. I was having parties every weekend because my mom had started drinking at the bars after the divorce, and she was never there to tell me, "No parties." When she did get home, she was too drunk herself to care or kick anyone out. We would wake up the next day to kids coming out of cornfields and sleeping all over. From couches in the house to the trampoline out back and in the barn. Wherever we passed out. I was the first of my siblings to graduate from high school. Thank God I was at least still there enough to do my homework during my addiction. I went on to college at IUK (Indiana University of Kokomo). I studied early childhood education and psychology. By then I was drinking daily and taking any pills I could get my hands on.

I ended up "fixing" my ID to say I was 21 and was bar hopping a lot with my roommate. She liked to use some when I met her, and I believe I turned her into a full-fledged addict. We were using more than going to school. I ended up losing my job at the daycare because my addiction made me unreliable.

I was so upset. I went to a bar one night, and the next thing I know I'm at Motel 6 with a man on top of me trying to get my pants off. I was reaching around for anything I could grab to fight him off and found an ink pen. I stabbed him with an ink pen, and he hit me and knocked me out. I woke up at a Motel 6 alone in a room, didn't even have my shoes. They had stolen my car and everything. I didn't go to the hospital because I felt like it was my own fault.

After losing my job and my car, I then lost my school funding and apartment because I didn't have a car, and I was too deep into depression and addiction. I moved back in with my mom and joined the Army. I was hoping the Army would straighten me out. I went to become a signal support systems specialist. I was to work on satellite communications. I went to boot camp by the grace of God because I had the flattest feet I have ever seen. God put me there for a reason because I ended up learning some self -discipline and was eventually discharged because of my feet. But, I was there for mom when Ray committed suicide.

I started working security at a factory and at a gas station for a while before I moved back to Kokomo. When I got back to Kokomo, I eventually moved in with my sister. I started going to Ivy Tech trying to

do the Early Childhood education again. My mom and
brother had taken off to Texas trying to run from her
problems, so my sister and I had each other to cling
to. We grew in our friendship and sisterhood so much
living together. I ended up dropping out of college
again because I was too much into my addictions and
party life style. My sister ended up getting married,
and I had to move in with my mom and brother. By
this time I had been drug tested at the Village Pantry
and lost my assistant manager job.

I started working at Walgreens and got health
insurance. I found out I have severe herniated and
ruptured discs in my back. I used my insurance to get
pain pills from the doctor and got severely hooked on
Oxycontin and Lortabs. I was drinking and taking
meds everyday all this time, and my life was kind of a
blur. I was working at Walgreens still, but my
addictions were showing. It was obvious I had a
problem, and they fired me the first chance they could.

Since I lost my insurance, I lost my pills. I started
going to the Methadone clinic on my unemployment
money. I was always nodding out, and I am so lucky I
didn't catch the house on fire. I would live just to use
and forget. Eventually I was arrested on the way to
the clinic because I was driving erratically and had
weed in the car. Thank God I didn't kill anyone while
driving back and forth to the clinic. I spent only one
day in jail because I was withdrawing so severely from
Methadone, they released me the next day. I don't
remember much after that until I attempted suicide. I
took a bottle of Ativan and Box of Benadryl.

After grandma passed away, I tried rehab at the
YWCA in Northern Indiana. I only stayed there a few
weeks because I was sneaking around and using every
chance I could. I ended up getting kicked out and
moving to a domestic violence shelter in Warsaw,
Indiana. I was clean when I went in but ended up with
the opportunity to drink and my drinking spiraled out
of control again. I was going into a Marsh there in
Warsaw and walking out with a Fifth of vodka a few

times a week. I know they had to smell it on me at the
shelter, but for some reason they never kicked me out.
I stayed there forty-five days and ended up moving
back to Kokomo with my mom. My cousin was into
cooking Meth at that time, so I jumped on that
bandwagon. I ended up dating a guy named David
who also cooked. I was drinking and
smoking/snorting Meth daily. I didn't do much but
get high and drunk during that time. I remember
being so high I was absolutely sure his family was out
to kill me.

Meth is a crazy drug, I knew I was hallucinating, but I
couldn't talk myself out of what I was hearing. I was
lying in bed trying to sleep, and I swore I heard his
dad spread a tarp in the kitchen and say, "It's time." I
grabbed my knife and made sure I could reach it and
just lied there till I fell asleep finally. It was such a
crazy drug. I loved how I felt for about an hour, but
then for about the next 6-12, I felt awful and just
wanted to sleep or use more so I didn't feel terrible.
Meth is the only drug I was able to just put down and
walk away from because it was so horrible.

I ended up breaking up with David because he
couldn't stop using, and I went to live at a horse ranch
in Logansport, Indiana. I was in training to lead trail
rides and work in the barns. I was living in an
apartment on the ranch and loved it! I was still
drinking everyday though, and that was an issue. I
stayed there for about a month and a half before my
boss fired me because he was worried about my
drinking. I miss that job so much. It was by far the
most favorite job I ever had.

When I left there on the last day, I ended up driving
straight to a bar. Everything I owned was in my car,
and I had no idea where I was going to even stay that
night. I met a man named Michael who was a truck
driver. He offered me to stay the night and to ride to
Chicago with him the next day. It's crazy, but I
actually said yes. I am so lucky he wasn't a maniac
murderer or rapist. I was so drunk and out of it even

when I woke up at this strange man's house the next day, I was still so out of it. I didn't have the sense to be scared. We drove to Chicago, and I had him stop on the way to get me another fifth because I had the shakes and was starting to feel sick. It's crazy, but I ended up moving in with him. We got together, and he put up with my crazy drinking antics. I still had a car at this time, but probably shouldn't have because I was so drunk most of the time.

We lived above his family's bar, and I drank everyday while he drove his big rig. I eventually got arrested for a P.I. (Public Intoxication) and spent twenty-eight days in jail because of a probation violation. That was the longest I had ever spent in jail. I am so lucky I never wrecked and hurt myself or anyone else. I sold my car to help my mom out with the rent back in Kokomo.

Mike always wanted me to go on the road with him, and I wanted to travel but my addiction made it very hard. I ended up on the road with him for a week and was losing my mind with boredom. I was sober and realized how much I didn't want to marry this man that I had said yes to in a drunken stupor. It was our one-year anniversary, and we were at a truck stop in Indy at a bar. He yet again didn't even get me so much as a card for the holiday (I never received Birthday, Christmas, Valentine's Day cards, nothing!) I was drinking, and decided I couldn't be in his truck with him for even one more minute! I met another guy at the bar we were at, and he was staying in a hotel room. I asked him if he could get me back to Kokomo and he said yes. Again by the grace of God, he wasn't some psycho killer. I stayed drunk with him for about three days, and he bought me a bus ticket back to Kokomo.

Kokomo was like a black hole of bad influences that kept sucking me back in. I moved back in with my mom and was stealing alcohol from stores and drinking all the time. I was hanging out with trashy people in trashy places.

I met a man whose uncle was dying from bone cancer. We will call him. G. G was an older black man doing his best trying to take care of his uncle. G didn't have much medical knowledge, nor did he have much emotional control when he would get upset. He asked me to move in and help take care of his uncle. He would give me a Morphine or two a day, and most days would go get me a few beers. His uncle loved me to death, and I loved that poor man too. I ended up taking care of him when there was a huge flood in Kokomo. I think the Lord put me there to make sure he got out of the house and into a nursing home safely. The water was waist high. I had to put him on a dingy to get him out and to an ambulance to get to the nursing home.

G was nowhere in sight, and I didn't know where he was or how to reach him. I stayed back in order to be there when G finally came home. He had two handguns that he always carried. When he got back, we had to leave the apartment obviously because of all the water. We stayed at a gym full of people for a week while trying to find a new place to get his uncle back home. He didn't want to carry the guns while in the gym so he had me put them both in my coat pockets that whole week. I thank God I didn't get caught with them or worse, him ask me to use them. We finally got a new place and got his uncle back in there to live out the rest of his days at home. He passed peacefully in his sleep a few months later.

I met another alcoholic named Shawn, and thought I fell in love. He was so very verbally abusive when he was drunk so I should have seen it coming. One night he had used Meth (that crazy drug), and I couldn't stand to be in the same room with him. By this time my mom was angry with me for being with an abuser and had kicked me out. I decided to sleep in the living room to stay away from him. I was laying in a recliner singing to my music with my eyes closed, and he woke me up to a baseball bat across my feet. He lost it because of the Meth and thought I had another man in his house. He must have been hallucinating because he said he heard voices. I called my mom crying, and she unlocked the door for me to get in.

After I left Shawn that time I kept drinking and going back to him. My mom said it was my low self-worth. I think it was because I truly did love that man. Even though he and his family treated me terribly at times, I didn't think I deserved any better because of my continuous drinking. Yeah, I would get sober, leave Shawn, then he'd get sober and beg me to come back. Every time I went back he would go a few weeks then would bring home another bottle, and we would be drinking like crazy all over again. Always a roller coaster. I was sleeping wherever I could because my mom didn't want me there anymore because of my drinking. Shawn kept kicking me out because he was drunk.

I knew I didn't want to live that way and was so very tired of that life, but I had tried so many times before to quit and stay clean and sober. I didn't believe I could do it. I knew I was better than the life I was living. God put me here to help others, but how could I do that if I couldn't even help myself? Finally around February of 2015, I couldn't do it anymore and yet again checked myself into the hospital for Detox. It was awful, and I was so very sick like I had been time and time before that. But I just prayed that it would be the last time. I had no Idea where I would go when I left or how, I just knew the first step was Detox.

My father and I spoke about once every few months. He and I were still distanced from each other. It was arranged by the hospital for him to pick me up and take me to Fairbanks in Indianapolis. When we got there, they wanted $10,000 up front. I didn't have it and told my dad to just drop me off downtown. I had nowhere to go except back to another friend's I had made through drinking. I felt defeated. I was doomed to drink all over again. It wasn't meant for me to quit drinking yet.

Thank God my dad turned to me and said he wasn't taking me there. He would take me to his house. We didn't know for how long or where I would go, just that if I didn't go with him I would drink again and I didn't know if I would make it out alive this time. He and my step-mom found the Wheeler Mission through an organization. The program at Wheeler is called Higher Ground. It is an 8-month program that is Faith-based. I believe it is my last chance at life. I have been here since May 12th and pray to God every day to thank him for sparing me. There are so many wonderful women here who have amazing stories and help keep me strong. It's not always a good day, but here I know I have a fighting chance and can persevere hopefully to show my family, who still use, that it's so much better on this side of sobriety and to please come join me.

Thank you for listening to my story, I hope it will help at least one other person realize that there is hope no matter what you've been through.

Editor's Note: Sadly, Sara left the Higher Ground Addiction Recovery Program at Wheeler Mission in early July. This is the only part of her story. She was an avid writer. We miss her words. We miss her. And we pray that she is continuing to fight for her hopes and dreams.

Sara Rose
Barbara McLaughlin, Volunteer

There is something about your name—Sara Rose. It's
beautiful and melodic, like Rosemary, your
grandmother's. I envision you as a pink-cheeked
newborn, freshly named for her, with petal soft skin
and a tender heart just bursting to give itself away.
Great promise lies dormant in your fragile nature and
fierce desire to love. Yet, something goes awry in the
garden, and instead of unfolding in your own time,
you are hurried, bruised, and repeatedly trampled on.

I met you only a few times, but you helped me glimpse
your life through piercing written details and the
plainspoken sound of your voice. You took me inside
your family's violent, drug-filled home, your breaking
heart as you watched your loved ones die; and your
conflicted, craving addict's mind. You've admitted
doing unconscionable things, but in my book, your
tender heart still trumps your crimes.

The portrait shoot was the last time I saw you. I felt
like a proud mom, watching you sit and pose. Your
hair was shiny brown against your black tank top. I
took your notebook home to transcribe it for your
chapter. Your words were written longhand with
lovely, fluid curls. I felt a sense of optimism, fueled by
the happy ending of your story, and your desire to
relate it in hopes of helping others.

Then I learned you'd left Wheeler. And your stories
nearly disappeared, too.

Please know your words are meant for this book—as
you are meant for this world. You, with the beautiful
name and tender heart. You, with the scars and
bruises and cravings. You, the writer, whose brutal
stories *must* be told so that children can be saved, and
broken people can begin anew. You're a rare and
valuable beauty, Sara Rose—greater than the sum of
your thorns.

Dying To Live
TyAnna Thompson

Life has never been easy for someone like myself.
Each year felt like I was being dragged into a deeper
form of Hell.
It started the day that my father left.
I was only 3.
It was the day that I became the black sheep.
To make up for his mistakes my mother bought me
everything
But she was hardly there. Made it hard to remember
her first name
When I got into first grade a part of me began to
change
Ms. Massy had soft skin so I gave her a card on
Valentine's Day
When I wasn't drawing stick people, Football was my
favorite game
Most days of the week, I hung out with my
grandmother.
She had an anointed soul, unlike no other.
She taught me how to pray and to sing for the Lord
And that no matter how difficult things were, He is
never far.
Her home smelled of mothballs and homemade
biscuits
Even though it wasn't a house she had joy without a
picket fence
My mother and grandmother lived in what people
called the projects
With tall fences resembling prisons that were meant
to protect
As I got older, I was able to stay out and play kickball
As long as I didn't bother my mother until night fall
I would walk back and forth to my family's home
through the cut
A fenced walkway and dying trees whenever you
looked up
Plastic balloons, needles and bags from drugs
Thugs wearing bandanas asking me to show some
love.

I would tell them my mother's name and they would step
back...
My mother owned things that could make the
concrete crack.
In middle school my clothes began to sag
And boys would call me names such as dyke and Fag.
I was upset because part of what they said were true
I liked girls and no one in my family had a clue.
My mom made me wear a dress. I would sing in
church
Everyone knew everyone so I was afraid to flirt.
The gossip would make my life even worse
I would never be able to love. That's what truly made
me hurt.
My inspiration, strong soul, was in for a fight
She had cancer and told no one until she lost sight.
She lie in her bed listening to the Christian channel
While we stood around her. I didn't know how to
handle...
The anointed one was dying
I tried not to, but even my tears were crying
She had always been the strength my whole family's
back bone
This was the first time I believed that God had done
something
wrong
Her long silver hair fell into her brush
Her eyes spoke...saying that she had lived enough
We walked back home, silently I prayed
Pretending everything would be fine the next day
In the middle of the night I awoke to my mother's
screaming
The moment had approached. I lie awake staring up at
the ceiling
Looking up to God, waiting for him to raise the dead
In my mind she was alive getting well in her bed...
We arrived...I was told that she asked for me.
I was the 5th generation, the last Thompson, she
wanted me to sing
I cried as I continued to sing the gospel song
Moments after, the strong soul was gone.

Life goes on, went back to Vine Middle School after a few days
Outside in line, a classmate called me gay.
I tried to sling her body over the wall that separated unleveled
ground and the track
as if it was she who had taken my joy and I was trying to take
it back
I got suspended and mother sent me for a switch
Work was something that she had no time to miss.
My brother, 3 years younger, hadn't know much had changed
I often envied him wishing I could do the same.
One day I broke down in class, must've forgotten
It wasn't night
Thinking of my grandmother, My English teacher asked for
me to write.
As my first page became 3, She sighed saying that
I had a gift in me
As depression sinked in my mother couldn't understand
She slept and took pills to fall asleep; to work again
Soon my brother battled his anger ...was attracted to danger
One time, he even gave my mother the middle finger
And she would punch him in the chest as hard as she could
As many times as he could take it as many times as it took.
I tried to get involved in Vine Middle. In my life it was vital.
I played piano by ear my mother missed my recital
When she would speak to me, I'd stare off into space
Wondering did my father and grandmother leave because they knew
that I was gay?
Could I bring either of them back if I tried to be straight?
Is life supposed to be this hard because I was born the wrong race?!
Then the tears would fall.

Mother would call me stupid and tell me not to come out of my
room at all…
So I would write and draw till blisters formed and reality would fade.
That was the life I lived my entire 8th grade.
The same summer, my mother started to hit me often,
I would wish it was her instead of my grandmother in the coffin
Then she would turn around and buy me things
While I blew them up with bottle rockets
All of my dolls were missing arms, legs, and eye sockets
Randomly I would ask, Can you buy my father back?
She would talk about how he was no good and he was on crack.
In High School, I learned that there were people like me!
I wasn't the only one with a complex sexuality.
My mother still made me wear tight jeans and
try to set me up with any "good looking" boy walking down the street.
Compared me to how the other girls dressed at my school,
Not realizing they were pregnant……
What a fool.
I was a nerd and hung around teens that wasn't confined with materials, drugs, and sex
It was 12 of us. And I could never forget.
We would hack computers, and change A's to F's on the report cards
Shout out to those who bullied us! We were quite beyond smart.
When it came to homework, none of us fell apart
He did all the math, she did the science, And I did art
I had many crushes yet couldn't catch an eye
My mother bought my clothes so I couldn't dress like a guy.
I wasn't allowed to go to parties so I would say it wasn't for me
And would go to school an hour early just to have freedom to study
But it didn't save me from the beatings…

My mother was getting sick and to be home was sickening.
I learned to cook eggs when I was in middle school
When things weren't cooked to standard the dishes flew.
Our home looked like a magazine from the projects into the house
Anything that broke, I had to fix. Moved majority of the furniture when we moved out.
Little did my friends know, I was on psych meds
And cried most times in the shower and bed
One day my mother hit me with a belt buckle on the left side of my head
The extension cord wrapped around a switch left my arms and back red…
It was the price I paid for running away
When she had hit me for not ironing my clothes correctly earlier that day.
My friends hated my mother so they NEVER came over
When they saw how bruised I stayed and my scarless brother.
The last year my mother knew I was good for nothing
She compared me to my dad called me a whore then more cussing
Missed my piano recital once again
The only people who believe in me were my friends.
I was only one credit short
To graduate and deal with hell no more
No one knew that I could ever sing
So when I signed up for chorus. I was deemed insane.
The girls that were like me were attracted to my voice
I started working and selling art to dress like a boy.
Knew a girl that liked me but lost life to drugs.
I promised her a date to leave that first love.
My mother was cleaning my room found a love poem
She asked if I was gay… I knew my double life was gone.
She yelled and screamed finally I yelled back.
You would've thought she'd be happier if I smoked crack
Like my dad
I tried to run there was only one way in and out.

We had bars on windows
And a bolted door in the rear of the house
She choked me as I began to stammer
Threatened my brother if he didn't hand her the
hammer
She aimed for my face as I blocked with my arms
Then on my back while I sounded as an alarm
Then on my rib the hammer nailed me again
She screamed at the top of her lungs calling me a
bitch.
I began to have flashbacks of me tearing for her while
she was sick
Cooking, cleaning, washing her when I was supposed
to be a kid.
Wore a tux to the prom
While the doctors kept my mom
Silver, black, & white. Hat & cane. Nothing was
wrong
While working and taking care of her (at 17)
I graduated and she was shocked.
In foster care I met my first and she
became my rock
Life became Rocky when drugs is what she sought
Again I wasn't enough, despite all the strength I had
brought.
While in foster care, it was nice to know that I had a
form of impact
The girl I promised a date to was no longer loving
weed & crack
She was in college to become a social worker
But my first had a seizure and I dared not to hurt her.
Again I was left taking care of someone who couldn't
love me for 3 yrs.
She couldn't determine her own sexuality.
So I packed… to run away and never go back.
At 21, my life began to make its own track
I traveled NJ, OK, NC from Florida to Atlanta
to see my other family.
By this time I was a heavy drinker & harder worker
Wondering why God would let me live even
further.
Everyone there was related I could tell by
their drink of choice.

My heart stopped when I finally heard my
father's voice...
Like my mother, my father was stricken with cancer
Amongst finding that he wasn't a crackhead and had
searched
For me.
I had gotten many answers.
Getting close to people, life has made it difficult to
handle
Back to Jacksonville, Life Is a Highway was my
anthem.
Then I met this woman she invited me to church
I proclaimed that God doesn't listen & prayers don't
work.
You know nothing of my hell, and I can't trust you
to tell...
But it felt nice to be of help & for her love I
quickly fell.
We had so much in common even down to my middle
name
She found it interesting that I could draw, play piano,
write poetry
And sing
I had graduated as chef with goals to have a café
To sell my books recite poetry and cook the whole day
We battled because she had feeling and would never
accept she was
Gay
Then I told her that I loved her we were inseparable.
We even prayed.
We, along with her 3 children
Wanted to escape
Her family trying to distort her children
Because we didn't live their way.
Suddenly their father wanted to come into play
Because he walked out for 11 years and didn't want
His children to be raised by gays.
I found a job in Indianapolis and our children
were taken
Because we were unaware the employer wasn't
licensed
Many laws they were breaking
Now this over talented author is writing

3 poetry books at once &
Is working to make sure that this hope isn't done.
Cooking and cleaning toilets whatever I have to
do,
To change the reality of this horrific view.
IF any soul should need an artist of any type
And have read this poem of my life…
I may be homeless but not by choice
I'm here for hire as long as I have voice
TyAnna Thompson.

An Unexpected Encounter with Poetry
for Ty Thompson
Rachel Sahaidachny, Volunteer

To write about Wheeler I might write about
expectations, even though I didn't really know what
to expect. Perhaps that's not true. Maybe I thought I
did know what to expect, and so—I wasn't expecting
to be surprised like I was when I met Ty. I wasn't
expecting to meet a poet in the homeless shelter.

Though, why? Because the poets I know are
connected to universities, or civic societies, or writers
groups that meet at Starbucks? They are often in
fellowship together, and I think rely on a certain
amount of communion with each other to thrive, and
to discuss language and ideas.

When I met Ty it was quickly sorted out to me that
she is a poet, because I am a poet, too. Her notebook
was in my hands within a few moments, with folders
filled with sheaths of lined paper, her poems
handwritten in pencil.

I held it, and I read it there in the mess room of the
mission—in the area they call the multi-purpose room,
which is a big hall with a stage and a piano and a
service window that opens to the kitchen where the
sounds of clean-up (pots clanging, large barrels of
garbage being rolled across the floor, a radio echoing
loudly and inaudibly at the same time) cascade into a
room of round white tables, where some women are
still finishing up lunch, and some women chat, some
women stare across the room into nothing, and some
women write hunched over their notebooks in the
writing workshop—and I was swallowed into the
world of poetry in a most unexpected place.

It is possible that a reader might find the trace of a
narrative in her poems, a story built on the expressive
moments of a life. But more than narrative the poems
explore emotions and relationships—personifying
moments of the heart. In her language she amplifies

plosive sounds, assonance, consonance, and rhythm to make the page alive with the passions of the speaker of the poem. She layers her voice with affection, with joy, with dedication, with questions, with rage tempered by surprise of language and consistencies of rhythm and in sound. Sound is a tool to get people to listen, and I was drawn in. Sound can create an almost enraptured state, and it is in that state that the words begin to sink in, and Ty's words say: *Don't make assumptions. Everyone deserves dignity. Everyone deserves love.*

Sometimes when I read Ty's poems, but more when I heard her read them aloud—I wondered if perhaps her big poet's heart, and all of her passion and compassion had caused her added pain in life. It is hard enough to be a poet in the world. Using the self as a way to reflect the outer world, and using images from the outer world to reflect the self takes skill, and strength, and courage, and, in my experience, a certain amount of environmental stability. I find it much harder to create art that captures the world with clarity in an environment of uncertainty. Ty is dedicated to her poems. When she spoke with me about the impetus behind her creations, or her latest experiment with words, her face was vibrant and her tone electrified by excitement. I marveled at the system she used to keep track of her collection. She had emailed copies of her poems to herself before, and she used her smart phone to draw them back from the cloud where they were captured, back into her palm, and then onto the physical page, by copying everything down by hand.

I know the poems will always be in her possession. I am so happy I was able to hear them. I know she will continue to write, but I hope she will also continue to share her poems. Poetry is of the community, and the many voices and experiences of the poet are how the language stays rich and surprising, and through this art of the individual voice society learns and grows. And, Ty, I hope you keep lending your words and poems to the community's ears and conversations.

Breana
Rise & Fall

Rise & Fall
Breana Rothrock

I Remember My Granny

I remember when my granny was diagnosed with cancer. I remember her going to the doctor. I remember the day that she decided to tell me, my mom, brother and sister that she had been diagnosed with cancer. We were all sitting on the couch, and when she told us, my first thought was, "This is wrong!" My brother didn't think, he just jumped up punched a hole in the wall and began to cry. My granny had stomach cancer. By the time they found it, she only had six months to a year to live.

I remember before the cancer being a little girl and saying often to my granny that I couldn't live without her, and that I didn't know what I'd do if she were gone.

I can remember her starting to have issues eating and throwing up often.

I remember the day my granny called, and I picked up the phone to hear her tell us she was ready to come stay with us. After many months of fighting cancer, she was too tired to do it on her own. I remember the day my life changed forever.

I remember the very littlest details of that exact moment. Like the wooden computer desk I was sitting at, the way it was positioned and the computer game—the Sims, I was playing. I remember the scared frantic feeling I had as if I couldn't get to my granny soon enough. I remember running to my mom's room and saying "It's time! It's time!"

I remember day-by-day watching my world fall apart as my granny got sicker. I remember the day she sat me down to tell me that my mom was a drug addict and was on Crack. I remember being so mad as if my granny was the one who was wrong.

I remember the very moment I was woken out of my sleep, my cousin saying to hurry and come to the room, and I instantly started to cry and was yelling, "No, No, please don't tell me!"

I remember being so innocent and full of life and once she was gone, my life had lost meaning for what felt like forever. I remember within months, I was smoking weed, drinking, and taking pills. I remember the day I moved in with my friend at age 14 and was introduced to and cooking Meth. I remember being so lost and addicted to drugs with no one who really cared.

I remember feeling like life was torture and the people I needed most was my mom, but she was exactly what my granny tried to prepare me for. I remember being so strung out and paranoid. I would stay up for weeks on end, thinking about my granny and my life.
I was 14.

Before and After Drugs

So much of my life has revolved around drugs and getting high. I am going to try to explain to you what I remember life being like before I became an addict.

The person I remember I was is somebody who had no fear and who was very outgoing. I spent my days outside playing with friends, making mud pies, and playing Pretend. I can remember how I never needed anyone to tell me that I was capable of doing something. I just had confidence in everything I did. I played basketball, softball, and varsity golf in school. I was secretary of the LEO Club and volunteered around my community. I went to nursing homes to sing. I hosted free pancake breakfasts. I passed out drinks for Iron Man competitions and triathlons. I helped build a beautiful garden in memory of a student we lost. I ran for president of my class and won all sorts of awards.

I seemed to be a pretty typical teenager, but little did I know that life was about to change me for the worst. I faced so many harsh realities once I lost my granny. The thing is I think I was already falling apart before then. My father was always drinking, and he chose to let it be more important than his only child. He soon went to prison for the first time, and I remember going to visit him all the time and just being so happy to have his love—even if it was behind glass or a barbwire fence. He was the best dad when he wanted to be; the only problem was he wasn't ready to be.

He filled me with so many plans and things we were going to do together, and I don't remember doing any of those things. I just remember him being so drunk that he sometimes got sick and knocked on my mom's door real late and having my heart so full of pain because I couldn't help him. I would get him food, water and take care of him if he could not. I would cry and plead with my mom to let me make him a pallet on the floor. He was my daddy, and I just wanted him to know I loved him. Still to this day, even in this shelter, one way or another, I try to do the exact same things for him, but when is it his turn to show me how much he loves me?

Where Dreams Come True

I used to dream of waking up and not being sick from pills.
I used to dream of sober days.
I used to dream of being a better partner, daughter, and sister.
I used to dream of not having to have an addiction that controlled my every thought, feeling, and action.
I used to dream of actually being happy and having inner peace.
I used to dream of not hurting myself anymore.
I used to dream about being able to dream again.
I used to try and dream of a situation, a person, or a place that could stop me from using.
I used to dream about being a part of something bigger.

86

I used to dream about all the people I would help, if I could actually get help.

I used to dream and think… is there anything that will take this addiction away from my husband and me?

I used to dream of when the time would come that I would save me from me.

I used to dream of my redemption.

I used to dream of life without drugs and the needle.

I used to dream of what it would feel like to be happy again.

I used to dream of moments like this, days like today. But for now, I am working on making all of my dreams become possible and even make new dreams.

A Day in the Life of an Addict

This particular day was like most others. I was up for several days on Meth and pills. I had a new boyfriend and that was a great feeling to have him. He came over that morning, and I remember giving him what dope I had left and him hanging out with my neighbor. Something was not right with me that day, and I knew it. By the middle of the day, I was having a severe panic attack and crying uncontrollably for hours. My brother took me to a walk in clinic, and they gave me a prescription for Ativan. As a drug addict, I took the entire bottle because they weren't strong enough for me. I was at an all time low, and I decided that I was going to take my life.

I wrote a note to my loved ones and walked to a dollar store and stole a bottle of 250 sleeping pills. I went in the bathroom at the store and took the pills within a few handfuls. I ended up sitting outside of the store on the sidewalk and the reality of the choice I had made was setting in. So, in some form of my attempt at saving myself or making my family aware of what I had done, I called my brother and told him I was dying then I hung up. I started to lose my motor skills. I couldn't even think, because my body was shutting down. My brother called several times, and to this day I don't remember a thing but what I was told I said and did.

My mom found me convulsing and slamming my head into the sidewalk with foam coming out of my mouth. She said she put the car in park as fast as she could and put her body under me so I didn't end up with worse injuries. Not long after the ambulance came, my brother said he went 100 miles an hour to get to me, and he actually helped carry me on the stretcher to put me in the ambulance. I had already caused enough damage that would have paralyzed anyone along with severe brain injuries. I ended up in ICU for two weeks on life support and a machine pumping my heart and lungs for me because they started to collapse. The only thing I remember is some very insane dreams like being surrounded by doctors, my mom, my siblings, and my granny who had passed away.

The doctor said I was lifeless, but every time my mom walked into the room, my eyes would flicker as if I could hear her. I will never forget the words my sister said to me later, that when she walked into that hospital room I looked like what she imagined death would look like. She said I was so white and just laid there basically in a coma. I lived through that, and now knowing God my Father, I don't question how. He was with me then when I had no idea who He was. He loves me that much, and I am forever grateful.

That wasn't my first intentional overdose, and if I remember correctly, it wasn't my last. Close to a year later, I was, of course, still strung out on Meth and Opiates. I was still dating that same guy. We got into an argument a street away from my house, and I was so distraught. I couldn't even think or function. I had taken so many Somas, Roxys and smoked Crack and shot Meth along with drinking and smoking weed. I found myself in a place I would never want to return to. I was so upset with him, myself and other problems that I never even allowed myself to feel. So we argued, and I turned and left in the other direction, and he didn't follow. I remember contemplating what I should do with myself. The only possible solution at that time was to kill myself. Once again I took almost 200 sleeping pills and started walking down Front Beach towards anywhere. I hated myself. I had no idea who I was. I was going insane.

So I walked a mile or so until I started to feel my knees buckle and my vision and speech all draining out of me. I was dying. I started to projectile vomit on the sidewalk of a gas station and in one of the scariest moments in my life, I picked up a pay phone and tried calling my mom first, but no answer (it was like 6 am), and then I hesitated and I called 911. Within 30 seconds, I was in and out of consciousness. All I remember was trying to utter the words to tell the 911 operator where I was. I can't remember anything but being in the back of the ambulance and the EMT saying my blood pressure was 70/30, and then it's all a blur. I woke back up to a huge tube down my throat, and I kept throwing up all over myself. What had I done again? When I was finally stable enough to be put in a room, I called my boyfriend. At that time, he was all I wanted, yet I seemed to be the last of his concerns. He promised me if he was not at the hospital by my side, before I closed my eyes he would be there when I opened them. Lies. After spending two weeks in a crisis management center and finding out he was in jail and had been lying about everything, and that he was sleeping with my friend, I was devastated. I didn't know if I would ever get over this guy and what he did to me, but God gave me something far greater.

One night I was in the bathroom of this pool hall shooting 3 30's (Percodan) and this chick was begging me for my Wash (alcohol). I did my shot with my 30's and was on my way to do whatever my little heart desired. The chick I was with was walking ahead of me and had her hand out like she was hitch-hiking, and I was so embarrassed. I fell way back behind her. Needless to say a cop rolled by and turned in the next driveway right in front of us and turned his lights on. Well, I already knew what time it was and threw my rig in the bush. I also knew I had misdemeanor

warrants for writing bad checks. So after I handed him
my ID, I asked him if I could call my mom real quick
and he said yes. Well, knowing that I had a container
of pills and weed, a pipe and some dope, I hoped my
mom sensed my urgency, and she did. She and my dad
were there in four minutes. She took my purse and
thankfully, the cop never searched it. I remember
crying and saying how sorry I was. Then I went to jail
and experienced my first detox in Bay County, hardly
waking up for almost three days. I finally dragged
myself off my bunk. I was sore, sweaty and miserable.
I proceeded to make a phone call to my mom and to
my surprise they had put my money on the phone. All
I did was complain and cry for someone to come get
me out, but it was almost $800. My mom was upset
with me but I didn't think twice about it. All I wanted
was those pills that was in my purse.

Within a few hours, they were calling for Breana
Kopko, and I was off to the races, or so I thought. My
dad paid it and was there to pick me up. I remember
he was so sweet and kept asking if I wanted food or
candy. I was so ungrateful, all I could think about was
getting home to those pills. When we finally got
home, I went straight for my purse and noticed
everything was gone. I instantly started screaming
and crying and cussing. I wanted back my drugs
ASAP. Sadly for me, my sister had come to my mom's
and gone through my purse because my mom just
couldn't do it. I was infuriated and wanted to fall apart
and destroy everything all at once. My dad had only
been out of prison for a couple months at this point,
and the pain he felt seeing his one and only daughter
act like I did over pills was saddening. I was
consumed, and nothing could pull me out. My dad
kept trying to hold me and get me to calm down, but I
was crazy and hysterical and nothing he could have
done would have been enough unless he gave me back
my pills. I feel like that day was probably a harsh
reality of how bad my life had become. The fact that
he even still had a daughter to come home to is still
baffling—between overdose, heavily drinking,
partying and men, I should have been dead. I once

read something from C.S. Lewis that said, "Pain insists upon being attended to. God whispers to us in our pleasures, speaks in our consciences, but shouts in our pains. It is his megaphone to rouse a deaf world." That quote couldn't be any more true for me.

After living in pain, agony and heartache, you begin to be able to be changed. If I had never felt pain or sadness or fear in my addiction, then I would not have wanted another way. God has orchestrated a beautiful redemption out of all my mess and mistakes.

This process is slow at times and lonesome, but when I think about the bigger picture and how far I have come, I can't help but be filled with gratitude and love.

> And now these three things remain Faith, Hope and Love. But, the greatest of these is Love.
> 1 Cor. 13:13

My Husband

My husband has been the best part of my life.

And December 21, 2014, I vowed to love him for all of life and after. He is my best friend, and the person that knows every detail about me and he still loves and adores me. We have had our share of suffering in the years we have been together. We have been addicted and homeless and at the end of our rope. At other times, we had it all and didn't want for much. We have overcome obstacles that most couples would have crumbled just looking at.

My husband gives me inspiration to fight and the strength to do so. Even when my family gets me upset, lets me down, or is busy with their own lives, I am always comforted by the assurance that he loves me. Bryan is a once in a lifetime kind of love that I am so grateful to have been blessed with. He came into my life at what would have appeared to be the worst possible timing.

Little did I know that the Lord had huge plans for our
mess. Bryan does something that no other person has
ever done for me— he never gives up on me. He
pushes me to always try harder. He helps me to step
out of every comfort zone I know. He runs beside me
giving me encouraging words. He motivates me to
apply for the job that I keep doubting that I could get.
He reminds me every single day how beautiful he
thinks I am. He supports my dreams. He cares about
even the littlest of things that concern me. He loves
the Lord and knows how crucial a relationship with
Him is. See we didn't always have a relationship with
Jesus as our foundation. My husband has the cutest
sense of humor, and I always laugh even if I have
heard his jokes or stories time and time again.

It's hard to imagine life without my husband. We met
about five years ago, two people from completely
different states, living two totally separate lives. But
the Lord already had it planned out that our paths
should cross. If any of the people or events would have
been timed or happened any different, I may never
have met my soul mate. Bryan moved to Panama City
Beach not knowing what he thought life was about to
be like. He met a guy on the Greyhound bus that just
so happened to be at one of the houses where I spent
the majority of my time (the dope house).

We had no idea the ride our love and addiction was
fixing to take us on. It was a true fight and battle to be
falling in love with someone but know your own
addiction could be his or your downfall. Not having a
permanent place to call our own made things even
more complicated. We lived in abandoned trailers,
dope houses, beachfront condos—all while using and
shooting drugs daily. We stole from stores to have
food, hygiene, and clothes.

After a year or so together and living like this, the
best and worst possible thing happened. I received my
inheritance of $10,000. As badly as we didn't want
what took place to happen, it did. Our addiction was

relentless, but we loved each other deeply. To the point where we would just cry and beg out loud for our addiction to end, or we would die. Always knowing what was right, we did what was wrong.

We stayed at hotel to hotel. Changing rooms often in a frenzy of paranoia from Meth. The little details of day-to-day living that lifestyle are very hard to write about. We were so torn between wanting that next high and the pain of getting it. After a couple months of living in hotels we got an apartment, shooting up to hundreds of dollars a day in pills. A handful of other addicts stayed at our place. Cooking and selling and shooting dope became an all day, everyday, Hell.

Within just a couple months, we were on the verge of eviction and maybe a month later, we lost our place to live. The insanity that led up to our eviction is unfathomable. We went to a friend's house the day before it was official and the next day as sick as we were, we decided to rob our pill guy. It's so hard to believe that instead of going and moving out my belongings when I was steps away from my front door that I instead, chose to let my addiction win. I threw away irreplaceable things that day. Twenty-three years of my life was in that apartment.

Our only concern was getting to a bathroom and doing that next shot. So now we are broke, homeless, and have nothing at all. The sick thing about addiction is it is a good liar. I semi-convinced myself that it would all be okay if we had enough pills to not be sick for days. Well that was another lie, because in just two days after that robbery and walking out on all we owned, we were very sick and irritable with each other. We got into an argument, and I stormed out the door expecting him to follow me. He did not follow right away, but then he came.

We were both so sick and weak, and couldn't hardly walk a block. Somehow we ended up walking right into each other, and I remember just laughing. We laughed and walked a bit more until we came across an ATV, and we were so exhausted that we just sat in it without second guessing it. Well then our minds started spinning, and he knew we could start this thing with no key. So he did. We took off in this thing with really no actual thought of the consequences and no worries. How could we have got to this level of just not caring? We didn't even make it off of Thomas Drive. The words running through my head were "Bryan, please slow down." Seconds later, we hit the curb at a wrong angle, and I went flying several feet and suffered minor road burn.

I remember thinking, "Where is Bryan?" At that moment, I saw him pinned under the roll bar and unconscious. I started screaming hysterically for help. I couldn't get this thing off him, and believe me I tried. Fortunately, we wrecked right in front of a Navy base and with the strength of at least six men, they lifted it off his body and released his head from the pressure of the roll bars weighing on it.

I didn't know if the man I loved would make it. He wasn't responding, but he had a pulse. I had hope. He was rushed to the ICU, and I never left his side. Bryan sustained some serious injuries. He had a post-traumatic severe concussion. The guy who had been so strong and the one who always made me feel safe was now hardly able to speak a word or walk. One whole side of his face was burned deeply with burns that ran down to his toes. I felt so helpless because what had I done and what had I not done to prevent this from happening?

He suffered memory loss, but he had not forgot me or how much he loved me. I was so scared that he was just going to forget who I was. He never did. And he still hasn't. He is the love of my life. I was able to marry my best friend and the man God created for me to share this life with on December 21, 2014. The life we lived, the situation we faced together would have crippled most couples. But, the two of us are a team and are more in love then we even knew we could be.

Our life is still a beautiful disaster, but together we made a pact to get clean and sober. We knew what we had to do and we did it. So we left Panama City Beach, headed to Indiana to go to Wheeler Mission's Higher Ground Addiction Recovery Program for Women and Hebron Addiction Recovery Program for Men. Leaving behind my family was hard, but our lives were on the line, and I couldn't help him kill himself anymore, and I never will again. We have both been clean since April 23, 2015 with very high hopes for our future.

I love you my husband, Bryan Michael Rothrock.

Rise and Fall

My mom is part of my rise and fall.
I admire her for my rise.
I admire my mom for always being both my mom and dad for me, my brother, and my sister.
I admire my mom for her unfailing love and loyalty.
I admire my mom for the days that turned into months of caring for my dying uncle and my granny.
I admire my mom for pushing on through life after losing her own brother so young.
I admire my mom for her strength when my granddaddy died.
I admire my mom because she is the most beautiful woman I know.
I admire my mom for never turning her back on me even when she had every reason too.
I admire my mom for always being there to pick me up when I was in trouble.
I admire my mom for never giving up on me.
I admire my mom for being the woman she is.

But, my mom is part of my rise and fall.

My mom was more then just a mom, she was also my dad. She has been such a huge part of my life. But, some of her choices led to my downfall. I know she never intended to cause me any pain, but sadly enough that is just a part of addiction. I was once an innocent little girl in her spiral that went out of control. And without her realizing it, my innocence was corrupted and the young girl I once knew was now wild and loved all things sinful.

My mom did everything she could to hide her pain and addiction from us, but without realizing she also hid herself and all the things we needed from her as a mother. The truth to that memory even hurts me to think about. I live with regret that I could have done more as a kid to save my mom. Why didn't anyone help her? Why didn't I love her more then my own selfish need and desire to want my mom with me rather then the fear of losing her?

Truth is, either way, I had lost her. I watched this drug take away a little bit more of my mom every single day, and I couldn't do anything about it. My fear of being taken from her or her being mad at me stopped me from ever telling anyone the truth. My love for my mom is an unconditional kind of love. No hurt or pain she ever caused could have pushed me away to the point of giving up on her. She is such a beautiful and strong woman—despite her mistakes—I admire deeply.

My mom raised three kids as a single mother. She is a woman full of courage and strength. She showed me what LOVE and loyalty was through her actions. She took care of her brother and mother through their disease and suffering. She put aside her feelings and was so selfless. My mom showed me the true definition of love. Sometimes love is hard and conflicting, sometimes it is confusing and lonely, but the greatest of all this is the other side of love that fills you up with so much happiness that you can't even put it into words.

The kind of love that never leaves. The kind of love that puts others first. The kind of love that always supports. The kind of love that only Gay Lynn McDonald possesses to share with the world, and I will forever thank God that he gave me my mother.

What Would My Life Be Like?

The day that I no longer have the desire in me to use is a day that I long for. I don't want to be an addict, and I wish I never was.

What would my life be like if I never became an addict?
Would I have graduated with the class of 2008 and had my family all together while I walked the stage?
Would I have applied to FSU like I had always dreamed of?
Would I have avoided so much pain and suffering?
Would I have kids now?
Would I have a great career?
Would I have had the dream wedding that I imagined since I was little?
Would I have made choices that would have helped my mom's and my dad's addictions?
Would I have the same best friends?
Would I be attending high school reunions?
Would I own my own house?
Would I have not hurt people in such a bad way?
Would I be happy?
Would I know Jesus Christ?
Would I be a better person?
Would I have married someone else?
Would I be successful?

Truth is I will never know the answers to these questions. Instead everyday I wake up with all those choices I made haunting me. I cry out in desperation for God to change me. My wonderful mother was no longer the mom I knew. This devastating thing called Cocaine changed her into a monster. I remember when she was not using how I would pray that God would get her that drug, so I could live without fear of doing something that made her mad. The drug held such a hold on her. And then drugs took control of me.

You Are More Than What is Hurting You Tonight

I tell myself that…
A situation will never be your end unless you chose
for it to be.
I tell myself that …
Depression, anxiety, addiction— it's all a lie.
I tell myself that…
The possibilities are endless.
I tell myself that…
You are made for so much more.
I tell myself that…
You are loved.
I tell myself that…
It is true and possible for Him to take that part of me
that can't stop obsessing, can't stop replaying the
feeling of the needle and how amazing I feel within
seconds. I cry out asking him to remind me of the Hell
before the shot, and the Hell that comes soon after. I
can literally feel my spirit reaching out begging for his
help, help from this addiction.
I tell myself that…
You are more than what is hurting you tonight.

Suit Up
Rita Mitchell, Student Intern, Ball State University and the Indiana Writers Center

In a busy lunchroom serving as both cafeteria and multi-purpose room, we met. For eight weeks, two days a week, in a room filled with blasts of pots and pans clattering, intercom messages, and trashcans being drug across the floors.

When I was first told that I would be entering Wheeler Mission this summer, I did not know what to expect. I had an equal amount of nervousness as I did excitement. I would be entering a place that I have heard of many times, but had never once visited.

Wheeler Mission is a place that specializes in helping homeless individuals get off the streets and into shelters where their needs can be met. The women of Wheeler Mission have inspired me more than they may ever know. Their stories gave me a new appreciation and perspective on life. Each woman I encountered carried with them a lifetime of stories. I admire the writers of this book. It took a tremendous amount of bravery and courage to do what they have done. These ladies were heroic to write and share their experiences with the world. I love these memoirs, because of the how many people will read and be touched by their words, and how many people will relate to the same feelings, emotions, disappointments, and circumstances.

One young woman that stood out for me was Breana. Equipped with a beautiful smile, sweet demeanor, and shyness, one would never be able tell what all Breana has gone through. Her intricate retelling of personal doubts, family struggles, cycles of addiction, and longing for true love are remarkable to read. While some may have their own ideas of who addicts are and how they behave, Breana breaks all stereotypes.

Breana's sense of truth shines through the darkness of her addiction. Her yearning to change her life is what saved not only herself, but also the love of her life, her husband Bryan.

My prayer for these ladies is that they realize how much power they posses. Look at your past not as your destiny, but windows into how far you've come. On this earth, we all have a range of temptations, obstacles, and doubts that we must all battle in order to reach our destiny. Trust that your past has indeed made you stronger. Forgive yourself. Get rid of any feelings of guilt or failure. As many times as I have thought about going back in time to change my life, I wouldn't. My past is what has made me the woman I am today, and I love that woman. Never allow past mistakes to control your life. From this day, into all future days, face the monsters with the armor of the Lord.

Loss & Legacy
Francine N. Jones

I Lost

I lost
>my focus.
>my direction.
>the foundation that
>was built when I was a kid.
>my self-esteem.

But what I haven't lost is
>my worth in Christ and who
>he say I am rather than what
>others think or say I am.

I've gained
>A heart change.
>my confidence,
>my dignity back.

Leaving a Legacy

I want to first give honor to God and thank Him for
the wonderful mother he blessed me with. My mother
did everything to make sure that me and my two
sisters were taken care of.

My father wasn't in my life much, but I always knew
who he was. He was in and out of prison all my life.
He was a Heroin user. When I was 15, my father was
murdered. That was the most horrible thing that
could happened to a teenager, especially a girl. I loved
my father very much, and I know he loved me. His
drug use numbed all his pain and shame. For whatever
reason, he couldn't be the man God needed him to be,
or the Father I needed him to be.

But, I had the best stepfather in the world. God all the
way provided for me. I had a very good childhood. I
was never abused physically, but mentally, my
childhood was a roller coaster. I never knew how to fit

in, and I was always acting out getting in trouble and starting trouble in school. When I was 15, I transferred from Arlington High School to Crispus Attucks High School. I did well in high school. I even graduated at the age of 17 with my Cosmetology license.

At the age of 18, I gave birth to a beautiful girl. I named her Shanetra I call her NeNe. Other than God, she was the best thing that ever happened to me. At the age 25 to 30, I was working full time in a busy beauty salon. I did well for myself. I even became the assistant manager and was well-liked.

Then I found out that everybody in the shop was using, including me. And so it went down hill from there. I loved the limelight—at least I thought I did. I was at the club seven days a week. I did this for years. My drug use got worse, and I started leaving my daughter for weeks at a time. My big sister lived downstairs from me her, and her and her husband, the Ivy's, took care of my daughter.

I continued down this road until I was 42 years old living in my apartment with no light or gas, getting ready to be evicted. My nephew had passed away in a car accident and three months later, my grandmother had also passed. I knew then if I wanted to ever see them again, I needed to get my act together so I could see them in Heaven.

I called my friend of twenty years and told her that I needed help, and I was tired of this life style. She said to me, "Francine, if I can change, so can you." She encouraged me. She sent her daughter to pick me up, and I spent a week with her and her family. On December 27, 2002, I told her I was ready to get help, so we call the 211 help line, and they referred me to the Wheeler Mission Care Center.

All the staff was very nice and the next day, they told me about a program called the Higher Ground Program. I joined the Higher Ground's program on

January 18, 2003. I graduated April 16, 2004, and I even started working for wheeler Mission in November of 2003 and worked at Wheeler for ten years.

Around 2013, after being clean for ten years, I started drinking socially with some friends, thinking it would be okay. It wasn't, because then I started buying it. Drinking became a big part of my life. It was a necessity. All it did was give me a false sense of hope. I went from once a week to twice a week and then every day. My drinking lead to partying and drugs.

My drinking and drugs led to impulsive behavior. Alcohol was never my friend. It blocked out many years of my life, and I became dysfunctional. Alcohol and drugs stripped me of my self-worth, my dignity. Using drugs and alcohol is a recipe for disaster. Just like a dog returning back to his vomit, my life was spiraling out of control (Psalm 26:11). I knew I needed help and quick. I resigned from my job. I had to leave with some dignity after all. Wheeler Mission had been good to me through the years.

I resigned January 28, 2014 and rejoined the Higher Grounds Program. I am now 17-months into the Addiction program, writing my story to let you know that the struggle of addiction is real. The difference between the first program and the second one is my heart. You have to surrender all to God.

You need to have accountability in your life not only to stay clean from drugs and alcohol, but to just *make* it in the world. You need someone to come along side you and speak the truth in love. Before I wrote this, I lost my focus, my direction, my self-esteem, even my self-worth in Christ.

Through God's grace and mercy, I've gained a heart change, my confidence, my dignity, and even my self-worth back. In return with all I've lost and gained, I know if I had not lost some of these things, I wouldn't have surrendered all to Christ, wouldn't have surrendered if I had not been broken. By being broken, my God will redeem all my past and that will allow me to leave a legacy to my daughter and grandchildren of what it's like to live for Christ. Falling in love with Jesus was the best thing I have ever done.

All through my addiction, my daughter and my family have always loved me. They just didn't like the things I did. I made bad choices with my daughter, but we were always together until the time she was old enough to move out. She has always had respect for me through it all, good, bad and ugly. My daughter is my best friend.

My mother is my number one listener. My baby sister gives me hope. My older sister gives me wisdom. My grandchildren are the apples of my eye. My great-grand daughter is my future. But God is my all and all. He has taken away my fear and given me faith, taken away my shame and given me grace. My story is dedicated to all the recovering and suffering addicts.

The struggle is real.

Don't Start

I just want you to know if you don't use drugs, don't start. It will take you to a place you don't want to be. It affects a part of your brain that doesn't allow you to think about the consequences or who you hurt. This part of the brain is called the Limbic System. We try to convince ourselves and say things like, "I'm only hurting myself."

That's not true.

You hurt everybody who loves you. My drug addiction has robbed me of thirty years. Now that I have surrendered everything to Christ, He has and will continue to redeem all the time I lost in addiction.

I missed my only daughter's graduation. I can't remember the first seven years of my grandson's life. I was in my own world of addiction, but by the Grace of God, He has restored my relationship with me and my grandson. My grandson is my hero; his name is Jeffrey.

I have two granddaughters, Tanetra and Odyssey, and one great granddaughter named Mariah. There is nothing like family. I hope there is something in what I wrote that will make a difference in the way you view addiction and homelessness.

> Always remember to give an answer for the Hope you have in Christ Jesus through your Testimony.
> Peter 3:15

Debra
Wheeler Mission: Before & Now

Wheeler Mission: Before & Now
Debra Barnes

I Remember…

I remember a happier time in my life.
I remember my favorite cat Petie. He was a beautiful
and smart blonde and white cat.
I remember going to California when I was twelve and
seeing Lucille Ball's house.
I remember being baptized at age 12and the feeling
that came over me.
I remember being in college, having a boyfriend and
friends. Going to parties, going to football games,
eating Friday night dinners out because they didn't
serve a meal in the dining service.
I remember family get-togethers at both of my
grandparents' houses, where we celebrated
Christmases, Thanksgiving etc.
I remember spending time in the country in
Noblesville at my grandparent's house, playing cards,
drinking coffee, watching my grandparents work their
garden and eating delicious garden vegetables and
fruit from their trees.
I remember my grandfather taking us to Forest Park
and then out for ice cream. He would also take us to
the drug store where he would buy candy and candy
cigarettes so we could be like him.
I remember playing in pool tournaments and winning
second place a couple of times. I remember going to
bars and sometimes winning the table and winning
game after game and holding the table a long time
while guys and, sometimes girls, challenged the table.

Introductions

My name is Debra Barnes. I decided to include my
name with my chapter even though it's about my
struggles with homelessness. If I am going to be brave
enough to put it in writing—why hide from the truth.
I am in my mid-fifties. I am a Christian. I am from

Indianapolis. I was born and raised here, though from ages 9 to 16, we lived in Belleville, Illinois because of my dad's job with the government. He was then transferred back to Indianapolis where we are from. He is retired now, and my parents live in Florida.

When I was younger, I was very athletic and very good at sports. I was a track star in high school. I lettered every year and held the school record in four events: the 440 and 880 relays, the long jump, and the softball throw. I have always been a good swimmer, and I played softball, volleyball, etc. I was very good at Ping-Pong because I grew with a Ping-Pong table. I started bowling when I was in grade school. I was also involved in choir and drama club. I had been in some musicals in school and also was a homeroom representative. In my 20's, I decided I wanted to be good at pool. I bowled in bowling leagues for over fifteen years. My average was 155 to 160, and my highest game was 225. I have also played pool for years and have been in a few pool tournaments. I am very good, called a "pool shark" by many people. My highest award was second place. I have won money three or four times for pool.

In sixth grade, I won a spelling bee for my whole school and got to travel to St. Louis to meet Buffy from *Family Affair*. In eighth grade, I attended Central Junior High in Belleville, Illinois. I was asked to be one of two people to give the graduation speech in eighth grade.

My award in high school that I was most proud of was that I had earned more total points in sports (track and field) than anyone else in the history of the school. I got a special award for that at my track banquet. I attended Belleville West High School in Belleville, Illinois. This is the hometown of Jimmy Connors, tennis pro, and Buddy Elbsen, who was Jed Clampett of the *Beverly HillBillies*. Belleville had never had a woman's track team so since I had always excelled in the field days at junior high, I had always wanted to run track. Well myself and two other girls went to the principal, and we got him to start the first girl's track team Belleville West had ever had in 1973, and they've had one ever since. I was always proud of that.

The following year we moved back to Indianapolis in the summer, and I attended and graduated from Lawrence Central High School. They already had a girl's track team, which I joined. I went to Ball State in Muncie, Indiana for three and a half years and majored in legal assistance. I ran track my first year in college. I am not going to tell my whole life's history, but I want you to understand that growing up, I was very active in extracurricular activities and then after college (I did not graduate), I began working in the legal field as a legal secretary and legal assistant. My major was legal assistance, but at 23 I started getting legal experience at a legal clinic as an entry-level position. I worked in that field as a legal secretary since I hadn't finished college. I also worked at some law firms, and I also did a lot of legal temp work for different law firms in long and short-term assignments.

You may wonder why I didn't finish college. Well, I had no support from my parents. Even though they could afford to pay for college, they did not. This was my mother's decision. My dad made very good money as a postal inspector for the government. I couldn't get financial aid. However, my grandparents did pay for some of my college. I just didn't know from quarter to quarter if I would be able to continue because I didn't know where the money would come from. It didn't give me an incentive to try. So I quit after I became a junior. I also worked part-time the whole time I was there. And the experience of going to college was one of the best of my life. I have other work experience like waitressing in nice restaurants and cashiering.

My problems really didn't start until twenty-eight years ago, during which three serious things happened to me. One in 1987, one in 1995, and one in 2011. In

1987, I was in a serious car accident on interstate 70 in rush hour traffic. I was stopped and was rear-ended by a car going about 65-70 mph. The girl who hit me did go through the windshield but she was okay, just cut. I had quick reaction time and kept myself from going through the windshield by bracing myself by using my arm and foot strength. I hit the top of the car with my head, and I had to wear a soft neck brace as I had serious whiplash of the neck and back. I also had a mild concussion. I saw an orthopedic doctor and a chiropractor. They prescribed physical therapy and adjustments. The chiropractor said I had a partial permanent impairment. I should have applied for disability then, but I didn't and still haven't.

Then in 1995, I was the victim of a violent crime by a stranger. I didn't really feel like rehashing this, but it was a guy, who the police said, was trying to knock me out to rape me, or worse. The guy hit me with an object very hard in the head. I had twenty-six stitches on my forehead and it left a scar. I had a serious concussion but no bleeding on the brain or broken bones. It took six months before I got over the concussion, and it did leave damage. I have some problems now with short-term memory and for a while, I had trouble with speech. I am a lot better from that injury but my back and neck have been reinjured many times. I can't do heavy lifting, continuous bending, or pulling of heavy things or my back will be affected. Sometimes I can't even bend over.

I made another foolish mistake when I again did not apply for disability. After putting this in writing, I realize that me not applying for disability is probably the reason I have had problems, and is why I have lost places to live. I just thought I could still continue to work in spite of the medical problems and the history of concussions. In 2011, I had a mild stroke, which I believe has played a major role in my problems with finding and keeping employment and housing.
I come from a family with unsupportive parents. I love them, but they have never been there for me. They never helped me when I became homeless, and I did

ask twice. They don't even know I'm homeless now. They are just non-existent in my life, and have been for years. They got married very young and had me when they were 18 and 20. I felt abandoned by them at age 17 when my mother kicked me out the house just because I stood up to her. I'm sure this has contributed to my situation.

By age 34, my grandparents had all died except one. I have one grandma who will be 98 on August 4, 2015. Her name is Maralyn, and she is my dad's mother. She took me in at age seventeen, and I lived with her until I was 23. She was like a mother to me, and she helped me financially when I was younger. My Grandpa Ray died when I was 33 and was my dad's dad. My favorite grandpa, Grandpa Wayne, died when I was 17. Grandpa Wayne taught me how to drive in the country at age 12. He let me drink a little coffee, taught me numerous card games, took me to the park, and gave me lots of good advice. Grandma Madge died when I was 25. Grandma Madge let me live with her for the summer in 1980. All my grandparents were very good to my two sisters and me. My Grandpa Ray was a very kind and unselfish person who did a lot for us and other people. All my grandparents are Christians and my parents too. I know I didn't say much positive about my parents, but they did take care of us properly when we were young, and they did take us to church. This would take another chapter to talk about them, mostly my mother, so I won't. I just don't know them anymore.

My sisters, Betsy and Pam, are two of the most important people to me. My grandmother is also. My sisters each have two children. They each have one boy and one girl. All of them are extremely important to me.

So what I am saying is that three major incidents that happened in the last 28 years and lack of family support (my sisters and my parents all live out of state now), are the main contributors to what has happened in my life. I have had boyfriends, but have never found the right person. Now that I am older, everything is harder. Harder to meet people and harder to get jobs because of age discrimination. The old injuries have affected me as I get older too.

I hope as you read my story "Wheeler Mission: Before & Now" that you can understand how a person becomes homeless. We are not born that way. We are a regular person just like you, but somewhere along the line something happened. The amount of support a person has contributes to how successful they are also. Because if you have a job loss or can't get a job because of age discrimination or medical problems and you have no one to stay with and no one to lend you money, you will most likely end up in the shelter. I hope after reading my chapter, it creates awareness about what people like me go through. Maybe their attitudes will change and there will be more help in the future. This is my story.

Wheeler Mission—Before...

In 2013 I had a very rough year. I became homeless. I believe it happened for a lot of different reasons, which I am not going to go into right now. For now, I would like to talk about what happened to me starting in 2013 and why my story is titled Wheeler Mission— before and now.

In March of 2013, I was living in a sleeping room on the Southwest side of Indianapolis with my cat, Blackie. I had Blackie since he was a baby, and he is now almost nine years old. I loved that cat more than anything (except God). Blackie was my best friend. Everything we went through, we went through together. I acquired another cat while I was living in the sleeping room. I took a pregnant cat in and named her Midnight. The sleeping room was in a person's house, and I only lived there from October 2012 until March 2013. The woman's caretaker fed this cat, but they didn't want it, so I took it in and kept one of her kittens, Marcus, a beautiful long-haired male kitten, who is now two and a half years old. After a few months of living with me and all we went through, Midnight decided to leave me and return outside. One day she got out, and I never saw her again, but at least I still had Marcus and Blackie.

When I lost my sleeping room, I couldn't find employment, and the woman was going to sell her house and go in a nursing home at the end of March. I didn't have anywhere to live, but finally in April, I went to a shelter called the Queen of Peace run by nuns. I stayed there for three weeks, and my cats were living outside in someone's yard.

I was able to get some temporary work then at a temp agency working at the Indianapolis Motor Speedway in the month of May, and so I rented another sleeping room on the Southside of Indianapolis and only had it about five or six weeks. I couldn't pay, so had to move again. At least the cats were with me inside, not outside. I wasn't on the bus line, and I didn't care for the person I rented from. I was not comfortable there, but I didn't want to have to move. But I did. Eventually I had to put my cats in an animal shelter. This shelter normally only takes animals to adopt out but a third party helped me work out an agreement with the shelter so that they would care for my animals, and then give them back whenever I was ready for them. However, Blackie and Marcus had to live in cages. Actually they lived in the same cage.

First I went to Salvation Army, then in September 2013, went to Wheeler Mission on the eastside of Indianapolis. All the while, my sweet beautiful, loveable children (my cats) were living in cages. I was in the shelter from September 6th until November 18th, 2013 and hadn't gotten to see my cats since August 20th. I missed my Blackie and my Marcus so much. Blackie was also a large cat. Coal black with a little white on his chest and white underneath his belly. I used the time in the shelter to get dental help that was needed badly and long overdue, years overdue. I had two dental extractions. One in October and one in November. I needed two big teeth extracted because of gum disease and a broken tooth. These dental problems had caused me a lot of problems. I had dental infections many times, and had to seek antibiotics from ER rooms more than once. I tried, starting in late 2010, to find dental help but with no insurance, couldn't find a dentist to help me. I believe the untreated dental problems caused my mild stroke in 2011. I found out dental issues untreated for long periods of time can cause that.

Anyways on November 18th, my time was up in the shelter, it was a thirty-day stay, and they did give me an extension because of the extractions. However, on the 18th of November I had to do a thing called "winter contingency." This was where you spent the night in the gym on a mat and they provided bedding, but then in the morning you had to leave for the day until 4:00pm, then you could come back for dinner and spend the night. But everyday you had to leave and take your things with you. So luckily I found a place to put my belongings, the church I was attending at the time stored my things for about ten days. The day before Thanksgiving, in 2013, I finally rented and moved in a half double on the near Westside. The Westside was not the side of town I was from, but had lived in for 14 years with the exception of when I was homeless or renting a sleeping room.

I managed to find some part-time restaurant work, and requested assistance from my church in order to rent the half double, but I knew I wasn't making enough to pay my rent, even though it was only $375 a month, plus electric. But I was homeless and the animal shelter wanted me to get my cats. Worst of all, it was winter. So my plan was to rent the double and then find better employment so I could get out of the cold everyday and have my cats back. However, things did not turn out that way. The day before Thanksgiving I moved in, and the day after Thanksgiving I found a ride and went and got my cats. I felt immediate joy and peace, me my cats, my own place, with a stove and refrigerator, all I needed now was furniture and a better job. I did have to sleep on a hardwood floor in a sleeping bag for three weeks.

My sweet sisters, Betsy and Pam, who lived out of state after having moved years earlier, both bought me beautiful things. Pam bought me a used, nice couch, dinette set, and mattress off the Internet and my other sister Betsy paid for the delivery. Betsy had also bought me some Paula Dean pots and skillet, a toaster, blankets, sheets, lamps, tons of utensils, (all new) all for my new home for Christmas and my birthday, which was on December 3rd. I had finally told them that I had been in a shelter, so this was like the happiest time in my life. From that horrible year to the best birthday and Christmas ever.

The best, except for the fact, that I had gotten a cold when I was in the shelter, and I never got over it. In November, when I was in winter contingency, I also had two extractions and a flu shot. Being out in the cold and sleeping on the floor of my double in winter made my cold even worse. Anyway I became very, very sick around Christmas and was sick until March of 2014. I had to make two trips to the ER to get well. I don't want to dwell on medical problems but my congestion was so bad that I couldn't breathe and felt like I was being choked. I had flu symptoms and the hospital doctor misdiagnosed it as chronic bronchitis. It wasn't until the second visit that I received antibiotics. I honestly felt like I was going to die. After finally achieving what I wanted, I was forced to lie on the couch fighting to get well. I could not work during this time because of being sick. I hadn't owned a car for a few years by that point, so I went on the bus to go to work. But I wasn't going to try to stand at these stops or ride a bus when I was this sick. I probably should have called an ambulance.
I had liquid phlegm mucus, chills, aches, chest pain, and nasal congestions. I thought I had either pneumonia or a severe case of the flu. Being sick for this long caused me to get behind right away on my rent; but in April, I started working for a temporary company that put me to work in a full time, long term

assignment scanning tests and doing data entry in a warehouse. So my landlord let me stay even though I was behind on my rent because he knew I had been really sick. And he knew I started working and as long as I could pay every month, at least a month's rent, I could stay. So when the assignment ended, I had some work from them but not enough. By the end of September, I had to move again. I had tried so hard to find assistance from so many places and found nothing. I tried so hard for me and my cats to hang on to my double but couldn't. So it began again, the road to being homeless.

...And Now

When I lost my half double on the Westside of Indianapolis, a series of things happened before I landed in the shelter again. First I stayed with a friend from high school for about seven weeks. She told me I could stay with her temporarily, but later it was evident that she clearly did not want someone staying with her. She made my stay very unpleasant and hounded me daily about when I was leaving. I had told her I would leave by the 15th of November 2014 and that I did.

I made a mistake when I lived in the half double. I took in another cat and named her Shelley. She is a very pretty calico. She had hung around the double where I lived, and no one would help her. So since it was an extremely cold winter in January of 2014, I took her in because she was freezing. My other two cats, Blackie and Marcus, were neutered. However, Shelley kept trying to get outside and during spring, she ended up getting pregnant.

Then on July 14, she had the cutest kittens. Three were yellow and white with four little white paws, and one was mostly white with black patches. One died after a few weeks. But I named them Angel, the white one, Peanut, the runt, and Lucky and Lucy. Now these are all male kittens, however, I thought Lucy was a girl. I was wrong, but the name stuck. Peanut is my

116

favorite kitten. He has a round head with a lot of white on his face, which makes his nose look like a peanut. He is yellow with four white paws. He has always been the most loveable, affectionate one, and he's also the smallest and has been sick a few times. (I took him to the veterinarian, and he has had to be on antibiotics twice so far.)

Angel was very affectionate when he was little. Both of them used to sleep right next to me, Angel under my neck and Peanut by my head or body, or on the pillow. Lucky also is a very good cat; he had been very loveable. Lucy not so much. The kittens are almost a year old now. I know I should have found homes for some of these kittens, but I love them all very much. Once we lost our home, our struggle made us closer. When you go through something with someone, person or animal, they become more important. You bond with them.

Anyway, my friend from high school let me put my cats in one room of her townhouse, and I slept on the couch. On November 15, I only had a part-time restaurant job that I got in October on the Northwest side of Indy, where she lived. They were only giving me twelve to fifteen hours a week, even though they had told me it would be twenty plus. The temporary place had only given me two assignments since September, but my friend didn't care that I didn't have enough money or enough work. She told me we had to leave. I appreciated her help, but she did not treat me right while I was there.

My family is from Indianapolis, but over the years they moved out of state, so there was no one I could stay with here, so the only place that me and my cats could go was a motel. I knew taking my cats to a motel was risky, and I know it's not something a lot of people would do. But being a single woman with no children, my cats are a big part of my life. There is no way I could take them to the pound or Humane Society because that would mean I would never see them again. It could also mean an end to their life.

I took them to a motel that only charged $145 per week, and a lot of people lived there. I did not see a "No Pets" sign when I checked in so I thought maybe they were allowed. Later on, however, I saw on my receipt, "no pets" in small print, so I had to hide them because it was winter again. But a girl living in this motel told me other people had pets there before. This motel was horrible, but my heat worked very well and they had a microwave in the hall. I also had a big refrigerator in my room. The freezer worked right but the refrigerator didn't keep things cold, so I could only use the freezer. Also the hot water in my sink worked, but not in my shower. It was very hard to eat and I couldn't take a hot shower, but I couldn't report any of this because of the cats. I usually would just get cleaned up in the sink, and tried to wash my hair in the sink because it was hard to take a cold shower in winter. We lived there from November 15, 2014 until the first week of March 2015.

My kittens were only four months old when we started staying there, and it wasn't easy. I had a fan in my room, which I used for the litter box odor, and I constantly kept them clean. In March, we had to leave because one night I walked out of my room and didn't shut the door tight, and two or three of my kittens were out trotting up and down the hall. The girl working in the office saw them, and we were caught. So the owner allowed me to stay until my next week was due, and he said we would have to go then. I apologized to him and told him we were in between apartments and didn't have anywhere else to live.

The way I paid my rent was that I had some work a few weeks around Thanksgiving time. Then in December and January, I had to request assistance from several different churches. I had to make numerous calls every week to pay for part of December and January. My sister also wired me money twice to pay rent. Bless her heart. I had quit the restaurant job, because I was getting next to nothing in hours, and I thought my temporary company was going to start me in a long-term assignment in January that I had even gone on a tour for. That company went on a hiring freeze, so I lost the assignment. At least I had gotten a few weeks of work at a different place. Then I got my taxes filed in January 2015, and in February got a $600 tax check and $158 from the state. So I lived on that in February and March.

On March 22, I did not have the money to rent anything, and so through word of mouth, I heard about a sleeping room that was only $50 a week and included utilities. I never met the person, but I took the room over the phone because the guy allowed me to have my cats in my room. This was a very, very big mistake. Out of desperation, I said I would take the room without ever seeing it. When we got there, I looked at the room. The door lock was not secure on my room because someone had broken in once before and broke wood around the dead bolt lock. There were two windows in the room, but the room was dirty and very small. Also there was no heat or hot water because the guy's gas was turned off. He didn't even own the house— he was renting. And he was in the process of getting evicted for owing a lot of rent, which I didn't know at the time. He was using the upstairs bedrooms as sleeping rooms to rent out, just to make money off of them, and not even giving it to the landlord. I didn't know all of this at first. I asked the guy when I found out he was renting if he was in good standing with his landlord, and if he had permission to rent rooms. He said yes, and that he paid his Landlord every Friday. That's all I knew.

So once again I couldn't take a hot bath, and now didn't even have heat, though he did give me a space heater. I worked two weeks while I was there in a temp assignment through my company, but we only lived there for a month. This guy lived downstairs in the back of the house, and I believe he was a drug user. I was afraid of him and hated being there, and I didn't feel safe at all. Then I found out he was being evicted, so on April 19, me and my cats were left with no place to go. I had no money, and I had to get out of his house.

So in the same neighborhood I found a house with a lot of shady trees and a yard, and a covered porch. The man who owned the house was currently living somewhere else, and he said I could put my cats on his property. He said I could put them there until I found shelter for them. So I put their dog cage and dog carrier on the porch and covered them. I put bedding in the bottom of the cages so they would have something comfortable and warm to sleep on. Then I put three or four bowls of water and their food dishes on the porch. I knew this would be hard but it was all I had. Maybe some people might think this was cruel or wrong, but they loved the shade and being outside. It was towards the end of April and it was getting warm. Also they had shelter from the weather.

This all occurred on the eastside of Indianapolis: motels, sleeping room, and now this man's house. His house was about three streets over from sleeping room. I have never been inside his house, and I was not living there. April 19, 2015, I was living on the streets. This was very scary to be on the streets on the eastside of Indianapolis. I met a neighbor, and he helped me by letting me spend the night in his car for three nights then on the fourth night, I went to a hospital just to be inside. Then on Friday April 24th, I finally got back into the shelter Queen of Peace and stayed three weeks. The good thing was my cats were pretty close, just off of East 10th street. It was a very long walk, but I could still go take care of them. Since they were living outside, I was spending a lot of time with them. They were only outside for three weeks because I was so afraid they were going to get hit by a car, especially the kittens because they kept trying to cross the street that they were living on.

A neighbor helped me by letting me get water from his spigot outside. He lived across the street and that was why even my Blackie kept crossing the street. Everyday I was having to walk or ride the bus first thing in the morning to see my cats to take care of them, so I wasn't getting a lot done. I was trying to go to a community center, also on East 10th street, to go on the computer to look for work and try to get help. My three weeks was up at Queen of Peace, and my cats needed to be moved. The three weeks my cats were outside, the man started threatening me to get my cats off his property. Even after he gave me permission, he just changed his mind and I felt like my cats were under constant threat of animal control. He made me feel like I was trespassing.

I have been looking for work but hadn't worked since April. I am still employed with my temporary company, but they haven't provided any work recently, which is another reason why I am still homeless. Horizon House, which is a day shelter in Indianapolis has outreach workers who try to help people. One of these people told me she could get me in contact with a volunteer who gets foster care help for homeless animals, to help their owners. The volunteer said she was going to try to help me. I told her I needed help for sure for Blackie, Marcus, and the four kittens. Shelley and Kitty Boy were rescue cats. So she took pictures of my cats and posted them on Facebook.

She called me a week or so later and told me nobody would ever foster eight cats. So she said if I would surrender six cats, she could find foster care for two of them, maybe three. I had made it clear to the Horizon House Outreach worker that I wanted my cats back, all of them, and that I just needed someone to provide a place for them to stay and give them back. They could feed and give them water, or I could come over and do that. She had previously said she would care for the two I wanted the most, which were Blackie and Marcus. However, after that the volunteer said, "Well if you are not going to surrender six of your cats, then I am not going to foster the two." She said she would, but she basically stopped. She was trying to force me to surrender my cats. So I told her I would find help on my own.

On May 10th, I met Casey, a girl in her 20's at McDonalds from this same neighborhood off East 10th street. I sat down with her and told her my story regarding my cats. The man whose house the cats were staying at had a memory problem or possibly more wrong with him. I told her that the man would one day say they can stay, and the next he'd be saying to get them off his property. I told her my fears about animal control as well. I asked her if she could help me. She said she lived with her boyfriend, and he had fostered animals before. She said she would have to ask Dave if he would want to help me. They lived together, and the next day I received a phone call saying they would help me. We talked, and they said I could put them all in their basement. They rent a half double in have a large basement with three windows. So there is sunlight, a fan, and room for them to get exercise. So on May 11^{th,} the day after Mother's Day, I found a ride in the neighborhood and took my cats over to this young couple's double. I didn't even know them, yet they were kind enough to help me because they knew I was in the shelter. One thing the volunteer did for me was she did provide my transportation to and from the free spay and neuter place to get my cats fixed. While there, I also got shots for the kittens, Shelly and Kitty Boy. Blackie and Marcus were already fixed and had shots. So my animal's home has been in Dave and Casey's basement since May 11, 2015.

I told them I would come over about four times a week to feed and water them and change litter boxes. On days when I don't go over, Dave does this. I have three large water bowls and two regular sized, and four food bowls, and I usually leave enough food out for two days and always fill up the water bowls. Most of the time I don't have money, but I am on food stamps. I receive free bus tickets a lot, but many days I have to walk to Michigan and LaSalle. This is where Wheeler is located to East 12th Street, off East 10th. It is about one and a half mile walk one-way. The store is about one fourth of a mile from their house on 10th

street, so many times I walk to the grocery and dollar store which is further past their house to buy cat litter and cat food. I also buy food for myself and sometimes Dave and Casey. It is very hard to carry these items, which include tuna for cats, dog food, and cat litter back to their house.

When I get there, I have to feed and water them and open the other two windows, which I can't leave open when I'm not there because they can get out through the window screens. Now that it is summer, I also have to worry about the heat. I am constantly worried that it is too hot for them even in a basement, because they only have one window and one fan on them. On days that I have to walk, I am walking three to four miles in the heat to care for them. I try every day when I see them to go do something else, like apply for jobs and go to the library computer, and I have a lot of appointments too. We also eat dinner in the shelter at 5:30 PM and have to be back in by 7 PM, so my animals do hold me back somewhat. Dave and Casey still have my cats and are not pressuring me, but I need to be mindful of the length of time my cats have been there.

As of today, I have been homeless three months. I have been at Wheeler since the third week of May 2015, so I am on a waiting list for section 8 housing, which I have never had before. However, one thing I haven't spoken of yet is what recently happened to my sweet little sugar boy, Blackie. On the day before the Indianapolis 500, he got out of the basement through the window screens. I didn't know that window had a hole in the screen and when I went over there on race day, he was gone. I looked that day and for weeks, walking, looking, calling his name, and clapping my hands. I even went back three or four times to look for him. It's like he's disappeared from the face of the Earth. I called animal control, and went in person one Saturday to the Humane Society. No Blackie. Animal control said they hadn't picked up any cats in that zip code. I talked to numerous people on the streets and neighbors, and no one knows anything— supposedly.

I really think in that neighborhood, most of the people just don't care.

Blackie was the kind of pet that he would always come to me when I would call him. I know if he could, he would come to me. He would never just ignore my calls like that. So if I believe either something has happened to him, or he is lost. Or he was picked up or confined by someone. The only other alternative is he doesn't want to come back. I am just heartbroken over this. For me, this is the hardest part so far of being homeless.

What do I want more than anything else?

I want a permanent home, where I don't have to worry about money. I don't want to ever be homeless again. I don't want my cats to be homeless again, as there is no help for animals who become homeless or for their owners.

My Future Plans

My future plans are to return to the legal field or some other office job. That was my major in college, and it is a field that is very interesting to me and one I would like to return to. I had worked as a legal secretary/legal assistant for 14 years, but it has been 18 years since I have worked in that field.

I actually have enjoyed writing this chapter for this book, and I really hope it can make a difference in the way people view people who become homeless, or, as I like to put it, "being in between apartments." I hope people will see that when someone loses their place, living life becomes very tough. When people become homeless their pets become homeless. Also their kids are homeless as well. I do not have children, but I have multiple pets, and there is no help out there for homeless pets. At least not in my city of Indianapolis anyway. I hope that things will change in the future. I hope people in agencies will care about the needs of homeless people regarding their pets, finding places or shelters that will foster a person's animals until they can get another place to live and get back on their feet with an income.

For women here, the need is extremely great for bus passes. A homeless woman would greatly benefit from a monthly bus pass. Right now, a case manager can only give someone about four or five per month. Then they are out until someone brings more in, which could be a while. I've been walking for two weeks now because I've been out of passes. But if the bus company would give a discount to organizations wanting to donate bus passes, a monthly bus pass would get a woman to all her appointments, looking for work, or wherever she needs to go, even if its just to the Horizon House. (Day bus passes are very helpful too.)

Also, there seems to be a lot of help with clothing through different sources but there is a great need for under garments (bras especially), and make-up including mascara. There are a lot of clothes and toiletries donated, but usually not make up, underwear, or bras. Women who don't currently have money need these things.

As for me, all I want for my future is this: to be with God, as Jesus is my best friend, and in a place to live to be with my cats, secure income, nice things, furniture, clothes, etc. Hopefully after I get back on my feet and I feel normal again, I would like to once again concentrate on my social life, which I haven't been able to do for a long time. I would like to hopefully meet a man to love and be my companion. One who loves God, likes cats, and who is not judgmental. After writing this chapter I hope it will not affect my future relationships or future employment.

A Wheeler Connection

John D. Hughes was elected to the board at Wheeler Missionary Ministries in 1940 and remained until his death in 1993. He was also a lawyer who served in

World War II as a legal officer for the United States Third Fleet in the South Pacific as an aide to Admiral William Halsey Jr. His duties included the arrangement of the Japanese formal surrender. He was a Christian and contributed much to Wheeler. He was involved in the renovation of the Dearborn house Hotel, now the Wheeler Mission Ministries Center for Women and Children's current location.

When I was young and working as a legal assistant, I worked in his office. He was not my boss; I worked for another attorney. But they did share an office space, and I would speak to Mr. Hughes everyday. He was only coming into the office once in awhile for his mail. Everyday in 1986 and 1987, I would read his mail on the phone. I remember seeing files and pages regarding Wheeler.

Little did I know then, that someday I would be needing Wheeler for myself.

Debra Barnes: A Future for Myself
and My Family Pets
Jessica Mayo, Volunteer

When I first walked into the multi-purpose room at
Wheeler, it was still a lunchroom. Women of all ages
and a few kids sat around tables eating from red trays.
The room buzzed with talk, laughter and the clatter of
used trays as they were dropped off at the kitchen
window. Eventually, most of the women, with their
offspring and bags in tow, left the room to reveal the
remaining few as the core group of volunteers and
writers.

Lunchroom no longer; it was now a classroom,
support group, and madhouse of creativity.

I was hooked after the first session. The women wrote
to various prompts and told stories when they weren't
writing. They had so much wisdom and heart to give;
it was a true gift to hear them out, encourage and
spell-check when asked. I was humbled that they
chose to share such intimate pieces of their lives in
hopes of helping and inspiring, entertaining and
educating others.

Over the next few weeks, the group continued to meet
after lunch. The regular meetings carved out a space
for a new community of writers to form; one that
transcended age, resources, and ability in which the
most beautiful, heartbreaking, funny and joyful stories
were shared. The writers came as they could,
depending on medical appointments, preplanned
group trips, and life events. Some came just once and
others came as often as possible.

Always well put together and with a ready smile,
Debra came prepared to each session with questions
and multiple pages of writing. She took her role as a
contributor to the book seriously as she recognized
this as an opportunity to raise awareness on
homelessness. She wanted to show that the women at
Wheeler, herself included, are people with a past,

present and a future, with family and pets, hopes and ambitions, and with the refusal to be defined by their housing status.

During our time together, she told and wrote stories about her journey to Wheeler and how hard she struggled to avoid homelessness. When she lost housing, she wasn't the only one who was displaced, her cats also became homeless. It was an aspect of losing one's home that I had never considered. I know firsthand how pets become like one's family members, but it never crossed my mind what happens when their protectors are no longer in the position to protect and shelter.

Yet, Debra always found a way to care and provide for them, often one day at a time. I was amazed by her dedication to care for her pets that continues in their current time of separation. She taught me about loyalty in the face of adversity that I'm not sure I could or would be able to emulate under the same conditions.

Through this unforgettable experience, I have a greater awareness of the struggle that these women and their loves ones, pets included, have faced to survive and reach Wheeler. I found that we are separated only by the barriers we perceive and are the same in a universal need for love, acceptance, and validation.

Thank you, Debra, and the rest of the women of the Wheeler for sharing the stories of your lives so that the rest of the world may know of your enduring strength and endless courage.

The Best and Worst Days of My Life
Jean Arnold

I guess that as far back as I can remember after school was out we went on a vacation to the Ozarks in Arkansas. Well, the next day was the big day. So off to bed, get plenty of sleep. Wake up raring to go.

It's here! Lying in bed full of energy; that energizer bunny couldn't hold a candle to me and my sisters. We are talking and planning and conspiring about our two-week excursion. I smell coffee; the aroma snakes from the kitchen to the bedroom; time to hit the floor and jet.

Mom and Dad in the kitchen making the family itinerary, we are like little jack rabbits in an open field, zigzagging looking for our favorite things and throwing them into a suitcase, then stop. Our ears go up and we listen to see if we can catch a hint of our planned get away…then off again to throwing our things together.

My twin sister and I have the chore of getting all the water equipment set by the boat. Oh my goodness, we had life jackets, skis, ropes, gas tank and all the paraphernalia. Like Santa's list we check it twice. If you forget any one of Dad's priorities, you were in big trouble. I mean prison would have been easier on a body than miss one thing on his list!

Mom and my little sister, a year younger than me, had to pack groceries, go to the bank, get medical supplies because at ages 11 and 12, you never know what kind of mysteries and predicaments girls at large can get into. Everyone going in fifteen directions, yellow light, red light, and go! Dad and one girl in the truck pulling the boat, and Mom and the other two girls in the car. We are off!

We drive for what seemed like eternity. Lord, don't have to potty. Think of other things, but don't think about waterfalls, running water, or laughing too hard.

Just then, we pull over for a break. Throw open the door and run like a mad man to the restroom. Relief! Then inside the gas station store to get a prize, pay for the gas, and off again.

The last leg. Hoping it won't be long now. I smell gasoline and exhaust from the motors, the sounds of laughing and the kids feet hitting the ground, like wild horses on a round up. We pull in to find our camp area, jump out, and start setting up. Sweat rolling off your face. Screaming kids, yells from friends you've made, jibber jabber everywhere.

Finally all is set up, and we have free time. We are released from our prison, but are still on parole. The last thing we hear is, "You better be back every two hours!" Off we go to the old water pump well in the center of the camp. You're not cool unless you rally at the pump to meet all your friends. Look I say quiet as a whisper, "There comes Buddy and some of his friends." We were in love. One was worldly. Seventeen years old, shoulder length hair, shorts and a t-shirt. I had died and gone to heaven.

The sun is scorching our skin, it's red as steamed lobsters, but we were off to the swimming area. Run, jump, scream! Oh what fun. We swim around the inlet and come up and start all over again— run, jump, scream!

The roar of the campfires and embers flying tells us time to head back to camp. We smell something familiar meat on the griddle. Hamburgers! Lord, love a duck, our favorite food. We eat like little pigs, shoveling food, so we can scurry off one last time, one quick trip to the pump. Buddy's there with his friends. Oh the sound of love; at least I thought. We talked, we laughed, and we made plans for the next day. Darkness falls, fireflies glow, so off to camp. Of course, we got the third degree from the police officers (our parents). We all were tired, so off to our cots. The smell of the lake and with the fires burning, we drift to oblivion till morning.

The Worst Day of my Life: Extreme Grief

What is extreme grief? Is it the hurt and pain that one feels, or is the way you feel after you do something that hurts someone to their soul? Guess that one is as bad as the other. My life has been filled with more grief than one's heart should have to take, but I suppose God has his reasons for putting *it* on us. The things I've done in my life have not always been for the good of God, but for the good of me.

I imagine my first really extreme grief, beyond able to bear, was when my son, Jody was killed in an auto accident. I bargained with God, "Please take me. I'm old. I've done bad. Don't take my baby boy." He was in college and had his whole life before him. But as we all know, God doesn't work that way right?

After the grief came, then I didn't really give a damn what happened to me anymore. For a long period of time, it was on. Anyone who pissed me off or rubbed me the wrong way was in for the "treat of their life." The fight was on! Then something in my heart quivered. The tears come down. I asked God to forgive me for my sins and shortcomings and please take the hurt and pain away. I didn't think I could go on.

For a couple more months, the tears flowed like water from a faucet. Slowly, but surely, my way of thinking changed. Slow, I mean like a turtle goes or very nonchalantly just like a snail moves in one direction at his own pace. Then my heart was yearning for something different. Was Jody around helping God? Was God telling Jody go take care of your mom? I still feel Jody is with me, or is it God that I choose to think of as Jody? Of course, I choose Jody, and keep looking for happiness. Will I ever lose my extreme grief? God only knows. Jody only knows.

Pamela
Why Not Me?

Why Not Me?
Pamela VanVolkeburgh

I don't know where to start. My life's been Hell since I was a kid. When my mom remarried, we left and moved to Kentucky. I became rebellious after the split from my dad. I remember being in kindergarten and putting my mom's pantyhose on to go to school. She was a bigger woman. When I got home she said, "Oh my God—what did you wear to school? You weren't dressed like that when you left." And that's when she started calling me Pandora—she still calls me that.

I was the youngest, the last child, and so starved for attention.

I was really a mean kid. I think at 10 or 11, I saw Jerry's Kids on T.V. I went to the library to get a bunch of deaf-mute cards. I used a wicker basket from home, put a blue bandana in the bottom of it and went door-to-door collecting money. I collected a couple hundred dollars. I got in trouble. When I got home my mom said, "What have you been doing?" She used to take a slipper and smack it on the chair or anything nearby. But she didn't hit us with it.

I was pregnant at 13. Mom let my 18-year old boyfriend move in with us after his mom kicked him out of his house. She told him to stay out of my room, but that didn't happen. I remember I got out of the bathtub bleeding, and my stepdad put me on the toilet. The baby came out. I grabbed it, took it and put it in a towel. But she was dead. He carried me down the stairs saying to me mom, "She's miscarried."

Mom said, "Something probably wouldn't have developed right with the kid, and God didn't want to punish you with that." I think about what she said a lot. I've had cancer of the uterus and a complete Hysterectomy.

My boyfriend went into the service. Mom divorced, and her new boyfriend moved in, bossing everyone

around. He was very violent. The day before
Christmas Eve, when I was 14 or 15, he bought me a
case of beer. He was drinking whiskey. I said
something, and he grabbed me by the shirt and threw
me into the Christmas tree. Mom said it was my fault;
I had a smart mouth. Nobody liked him, and
everybody had a smart mouth.

I moved in with my brother in Mooresville. Mom
wouldn't give me my clothes. She'd had her stomach
stapled and was wearing my jeans. I asked her to come
to Mooresville and sign me up for school three times,
but she never came.

I went to live with my dad. My dad was an alcoholic
all my life, and he wasn't doing as well as I thought.
There was no hot water, no heat, no electricity, only a
pot-bellied stove to make beans on. I remember
cutting the mold off of government cheese.

My little sister would come to stay the weekend. I
thought I was grown. I met this black man that just
got out of service. I dated him a while before my sister
got to meet him. She saw him hit me. She said, "If you
ever go back to him I will never talk to you again."
And she didn't, to this day.

My sister got pregnant and had a healthy baby. I was
jealous. I started doing drugs a lot, shooting up.
My mom wouldn't give me my Social Security check;
she was keeping it. A couple days before my birthday I
asked her for some money to buy something to eat.
She pulled up in a new car, she said, "I can't give you
any money, I just bought this car." The car was just a
little junky Chevrolet, a little piece of crap car. I'll
never forget it. It was burgundy. I was furious. We
were taking baths out of a wash bucket, burning
furniture out of the house to heat the water so we
could wash.

One boyfriend I had cut my clothes off and raped me. I
ran out of the house with no clothes and jumped into a
cab naked. The cabby said, "You get out." I pointed

and said, "Do you see that man chasing me with the shot gun?" He took off to the Village Pantry, where a woman gave me a shirt while I waited for the police. Sometimes strangers have treated me better.

I started prostituting, leaning heavily on him, CB, fighting with him, leaving him, and going back. I'm still fighting with him to this day. He was keeping me off the street, I was thinking.

The last time we fought, he bit me on my face. I have scars. Scars all over my body from him.
I still love him, but I think it was more the drugs— clinging to him, dependent on him. All the time, my whole life, I was drunk. I would leave him and go to my dad's. He tried to kill my dad. Shot at him at the firing range. But I kept going back. But when he bit my face, that was the last time. He told me, "Keep it movin', come back sober." Came back three days later, and he was on the floor with a stroke.

I'm still a prostitute. I was arrested for prostitution. Been a year clean and sober. I look at things different. Still prostituting myself for his attention. He couldn't possibly love me, because I don't even love myself. I missed my probation appointment, and I'm scared because I don't know what's going to happen.

I lived with my sister when I cut my knee, got gangrene, and it went to my heart. Then I went to live with my brother. Everyone kept moving me around until I was 18. No one wanted me. I moved in with him and his mother.

He's held me from a bridge by my ankles. He's put a gun to my head. He's beaten me on my back, on my face, he bit me all over my face, choked me until I passed out. No wonder I'm a nut. No self-esteem at all. I am an "Okay, okeydokey" kind of person, you know? He took me to his friend's house because he didn't want to take me to his house. Someone else was living with him. We hit it off, and I stayed with him for about four years.

Halloween night, 2007. He had hit me a couple of days before. He was passed out. I wrapped the phone cord around his neck to strangle him. I left. I thought I killed him, until I heard the brakes of the truck locking up. When I turned around it was too late.

My best friend was named Tammy. She lived with me on Prospect. I came home to find note pads all over the door from my sister and other people saying to call. Tammy went off with some Chicago boys with a bunch of dope. They raped her; they beat her. She escaped from the second story into an alley where they shot her in the back of the head.

When he run me over, that's whoI saw and who told me to get out from under the truck. She told me, "It's not your time. Get out from under the truck." She said it three times, like she was right in front of my face. I had 110 stitches. 82 or 84 staples in my head.Road rash scars.

When I was in recovery at Wishard, I had another blessing.

My room was smoke free—there was a big sign on the wall. No smoking for Pam. My sister lit a cigarette and gave it to me. I don't even remember smoking it. The nurse showed me the blue foam pad I was on. It was scorched all around my body. It was a blessing I wasn't burned. I just wept and told Jesus thank you, thank you that nothing got burned.

My sister don't talk to me that much. She accused me of sleeping with her husband. I didn't. She kept her kids away from me for about ten years while I was running with people.

I went to the old Julian Center when he run over my head. I woke up by myself. Everyone was gone. I woke up when they were moving a deep freezer. They said, "Hell, where'd you come from?" and they took me to Meridian. Channel 8 came and stayed all night with the camera.

I said, "What about those of us hiding from abusers? Get it out of my face!"

I was still recovering from being run over when I went to stay with my mom. She couldn't take care of me. She called my cousin in. I went to prison for prostitution and theft, then to Wheeler Mission, when it was over on Washington and Rural. I was on the program for eight months. I had surgery to have my ovaries out. I asked my Dad if I could come live with him. He said, "Okay."

When I left, Ms. Lisa said, "I'll see you again, cause you're leaving the program." And I wish she hadn't said it. And I ended up right back with C.B. I thought he was taking care of me. Buying me cigarettes and drugs. I worked at an adult massage parlor with a big wolf on the door. I did some crazy stuff to some perverted men. They didn't do it to me, I did it to them. It haunts me. And I was drunk all the time and on drugs.

This is the longest time I've ever been sober by myself. I have severe anxiety attacks now.

I was on the cane, because of my sciatic nerve. I was on the cane and getting off the bus, when the bus moves up, and I fell. Broke both my ankles, and fractured my shin.

But, through all of this, I have never given up faith in God. I've walked the streets in pouring rain, lived under a bridge, lived in a shack with holes in it. I'm here for a reason, but I don't know why. But I don't question it, because I wake up every morning.

And I hope that someone reads this and gets strength to stay with God. And to try new ways—because you already know where you've been. If it wasn't working for you then, it isn't gonna' work for you now. Just keep praying. I'm very blessed to be here at Wheeler in a bed, because I've been in plenty of beds that wasn't good.

My mom had a stroke. I've forgiven her for many things. But she would rather have a stranger come live with her than me. And I have never lied of stolen or disrespected her. She's having trouble putting her words together to make sentences.

When I got run over, it fucked up my head a lot. The whole right side of my body is scarred. My face is scarred, and my head—my head is emotionally drained.

I don't think I got a Christmas present for about ten years, except for last year, here at Wheeler. It brought out a lot of different feelings and emotions. I've always been a giver, not a taker. It's always been really hard for me to accept anything from anybody—because what do they want in return, what do I got a do? If I wanted something, I always had to speak up. And I realized there are a lot of people in the same situation, and I am not alone in this. I was questioning, "What do I have to do now?" and it felt kind of creepy.

While at Wheeler, I got to go to a Christmas party with my mom and nieces and nephews and brothers and sisters. They were all giving each other gifts, and I shouldn't have even been there. I felt lost like the Twilight Zone. But I came back and talked to Ms. Liz, a counselor at Wheeler, and she made me feel confident and not so alone. The loneliness was overwhelming at Christmas, new situations, new everything.

I was holding my dad's hand when he took his last breath. He went in the hospital cause he bumped his head, and they wouldn't let him go. They said he had pneumonia, and he died. We asked him if he wanted to be saved by Christ and he did, so we saved him. And we asked him if he wanted to go home to be more comfortable. And he said he did, but not his house. And he said he loved us. And that was the best feeling in the world to know that he was saved by Christ. It made me look at things different.

The Bravery of Pam
for Pamela VanVolkeburgh
Rachel Sahaidachny, Volunteer

I sat with Pamela at a table, and copied down her
story as she spoke it to me. Pam has dyslexia and only
went to school up to fifth grade, so I imagine the act of
writing it all down seemed daunting and unfeasible. It
is difficult to face the blank page even without those
added barriers. I wonder, too, if she didn't want to sit
alone with it—just her story and her.

She told me she felt haunted, but she also feels blessed.
Her story is a difficult one, and full of trauma, and
things you think no person should have to experience
in life, but people do. Pamela did, and she survived,
and not just physically, but the spirit of her, too. She
sat there with me reflecting and recounting the past,
and I believe that takes a great deal of courage and
self-acceptance. She trusts God has kept her alive and
will keep propelling her forward. I am really glad that
Pam has found sobriety and a safe bed to sleep in.

She told me a few times, "I was a bad kid, I was really,
really rebellious," and I wonder about that
interpretation. I think a child is not really defined by
themselves at such a young age, but by their parents.
Parents are the ones who name us, who define us, who
tell us who we are when we are too little to know yet.
And so a child who craves love, and attention, as
children do, and who is wildly imaginative and
energetic might be called by a parent who is tired or
incapable: bad and rebellious. Might then be called
Pandora—so then a child might be named after a myth
that represents the harbinger of evil in the world, and
a woman might grow up thinking she has nothing
good to offer the world.

Language has power and naming has power. It is what
we are doing with this book even—giving experience
a language by capturing each individual story in
words. I hope people have compassion when they read

Pamela's story, and know that the words we use to define ourselves and others do matter.

I wonder if someone who has never known love and has only known pain returns to pain. I wonder if the two extremes become confused, and if the question, "what do I live for?" becomes confused, too. For Pamela it is God's love that has kept her alive. I hope that she has found a way to love herself some too, and I think she has, by staying sober. I know that she has faced herself. She isn't hiding.

Pam likes to lie out in the sun. When I visited her again to go over what was written, that's what she was doing, and what she wanted to go back to. She is very tan, deep amber with tiny freckles all over her skin. "I could lay out for hours," she said, "but the sun was really intense today. I can't wait to go back when it cools off a little."

I think about laying in the sun—the way the sun bakes into the skin and small beads of sweat collect in the crease of the elbows and behind the knee, and the way the color red fills your head when your eyes are closed but facing that bright intense summer sky. In a way everything is erased but that moment, pierced by the heat and sunlight: a solid moment of existence. I wonder about Pam, laying in the sun, letting the light soak into her.

She asked me, "Do you think my story is worth telling?" I do.

I do—not just because I hope that people will have more compassion for drug addicts, or victims of abuse and domestic violence, but also because of the bravery she owns in sharing. I don't know if Pam thought it was a brave act to tell her story. She just wanted it to be of use to someone else, to someone who might be suffering as she has suffered. I believe it will be of use in that way, too.

My Greatest Joy
Sandra Bernard-Vernon

My first and only introduction to motherhood, I couldn't believe that I was going to be a mom. In that moment, when the doctor said I was already fifteen to seventeen weeks, I knew I couldn't go back and change the genetic make-up of this kid. I was lost in my sins of drugs and alcohol. *Oh my God,* I thought, *This baby is formed—made of alcohol, marijuana, and tobacco… and coffee.* Wow.

Being an adult, you know what type of an effect these things have on you. Now I had a baby in me. A baby that I want to protect and cherish, and now I have already done damage to the thing I love the most— my unborn child.

So for the next twenty-three weeks, I had to alter all the things that I enjoyed doing. It was really hard, and only through the grace of God, my son was born with only a minor meningitis. It was nothing that he had to be hospitalized for. God carried him and made him safe and made sure he was okay.

When he was first born, I thought he was a deaf mute because he never did cry, and I had a C-section, and it was after the twenty-four-hour observation that they found out he had meningitis.

He became the biggest joy of my life. This little thing that I had treated so cruelly—not knowing—was my joy. I tried to make it up to him. I was a 24/7 mom, and he was always ready to go. I had him potty trained and ready to go to school by two years old. He was a playful child; he had this motor in him. He went from terrible twos to atrocious threes. I was thirty-one when I had him. I started at Ivy Tech, and thought, *How am I gonna do my homework?* But you find a way, and he was always ready to go!

To me, he's my greatest joy.

What I (Really) Want
Jen Noelle, Volunteer

What do you want more than anything else? I
thought about the prompt we had given the Wheeler
women, and a few things immediately came to mind. I
want to finish our basement. I want to lose those last
ten pounds of baby weight. I want to get more sleep at
night. Materialistic. Superficial. What do I *really*
want? I want to do something that is both purposeful
and personally fulfilling. I want "our boys," who lived
with us for two months and now reside with their
mother on the near eastside of Indianapolis, to finish
school and break the cycle of generational poverty
that plagues their family. I want to experience a life
that doesn't revolve around my son's disability. I
could fill a college-ruled sheet of notebook paper with
things I want.

Then I looked over at Sandra, her notebook blank. She
couldn't think of a single thing that she wanted. Here
was a woman, living in a homeless shelter, who
wanted for nothing. Even after asking her a series of
questions and trying to provide some inspiration for
writing, she still could not think of anything. She
described how she used to carry expensive purses and
wear Etienne Aigner shoes. She talked about her
career, her friends. "That all changed when I had my
son, you know."

Yeah, I know. If my response had been a pie chart, she
would have seen small, but noticeable slices of
sarcasm, regret and bitterness. I gave up everything
when I had my son and am still trying to find myself
again. But her demeanor was different. As she
reminisced about the early days of raising her boy, her
face reflected peace and pride. I learned that he now
helps raise his girlfriend's children and still takes the
time to call. I marveled at how, looking back, she
seemed content with yielding her own wants for the
good of her son.

My conversation with Sandra stayed with me and reminded me of Paul's words in the Bible. "I know what it is to be in need, and I know what it is to have plenty. I have learned the secret of being content in any and every situation, whether well fed or hungry, whether living in plenty or in want" (Philippians 4:12).

I want that. I want what Paul described and what Sandra exuded. Contentment in any and every situation. It seems unbelievable that I would envy a homeless woman. I have *so* much, but sometimes I wonder if my life of plenty actually creates a barrier to contentment. When you have little to nothing, like many of the women living at Wheeler, perhaps it is easier to be grateful for the small things like special snacks, a skein of yarn, or a hand-me-down purse. Perhaps gratitude for what you have leads to contentment where you are.

Sandra helped me realize what I (really) want and opened my eyes to intentional gratitude. I can certainly be grateful for morning walks to the park and Friday play dates with friends and a host of other seemingly mundane experiences that this stage of life provides. Of course, there are still desires and dreams that I hope to one day fulfill; contentment isn't the same as stagnancy. Rather, it seems to be the bridge between aspirations and apathy. Knowing how to see the good in every situation and look for the small blessings of the present, all the while hoping and working toward a better future. And as I now endeavor to look for the everyday gifts of gratitude, to work towards contentment, what I learned from Sandra is certainly a place to begin.

Valerie
Strap on Your Seatbelts:
You're in for a Hell of a Ride

Strap on Your Seatbelts:
You're in for a Hell of a Ride
Valerie Roll

Life of an Addict

My stomach is in a conniption, Fuck, I hate addiction.
I need something in my veins.
I feel as though I'm going insane. Just one little pill
will quit making me ill.
Gotta go on a chase, so I can make it back to base.
How crazy am I for always wanting that next high?
You wouldn't know if you've never given it a go.
I will pull any tricks to get my next fix.
Lie, cheat, or steal. Not above any of that for a little
yellow pill.
Now... I got my pill so I can just chill till the next
time I begin to feel ill.
Chaos! Some would say.
To me? Just another normal day.

I Remember

I remember being fourteen and finding out I was
pregnant and feeling so afraid.

I remember getting a call that my little brother had
been in a wreck and was pronounced dead at the scene.

I remember staying up for literally months at a time.

I remember being forced to have sex for the first time.

I remember always running away from home.

I remember being a dope dealer by fourteen.

I remember getting expelled from high school.

I remember graduating from high school and college.

I remember being awarded scholarships at senior day
and barely being able to accept them, because I was so

fucked up.

I remember our wedding day and the plane ride for our honeymoon.

I remember the day my whole world crumbled.

I remember shooting up that first time.

I remember people overdosing and dying right before my eyes.

I remember being homeless and feeling so alone.

I remember just all the craziness and chaos in my life these last 22 years...

I don't remember my daddy passing away.

I remember all the people I've done so wrong.

I remember all the bad relationships I've been in.

I remember the day I finally found my true love.

I remember every time I've been arrested and done jail/prison time.

I remember my worst black out, around 18 hours-- remember leaving friend's house--next morning being woke up by state cops but can remember nothing in between.

I remember overdosing three times and always pulling out of it on my own (God).

I remember all the hearts I've broke, along my life journey: daughters, friends, family, boy/girlfriends.

I remember being six hours away from home and going into labor with my second child.

I remember being completely strung out while pregnant with my youngest.

I remember finally after 18 years of being an addict, finally reaching that point of no return when I cared about nothing or no one, not even myself--only cared about the needle and my high.

I remember the DEA and drug task force coming in and having machine guns at not only my head but my four-year-old daughter's head too.

I remember my entire life feeling like two completely different people in one body.

I remember all my vacations, some pleasant--some crazy.

I remember stealing my brother's car in LA to go to Mexico to traffic drugs back, then being so wild on the way back that I wrecked it and ran from the police thousands of miles away from home.

I remember being in Puerta Vallarta, going places I'm lucky to have ever returned alive from for drugs.

I remember getting drugged on my honeymoon and losing my mind.

I remember going to jail on my daughter's 16th birthday.

I remember my mom going to federal prison.

I remember getting the news I was coming here.

How I Ended Up at Wheeler Mission

Sit down and strap on your seatbelt 'cause you're in for one hell of a ride when you read this.

The summer of sixth grade, my life drastically changed and has been craziness and chaos for the past twenty-one years now. Started hanging out with a different crowd, rebelling, and was introduced to the sex, drugs, and rock-n-roll lifestyle—and I must say, I loved the excitement of it all.

Like I said before now, for the past twenty-one years, I never looked back until now at age 34. By the time I hit 14, I had run away from home more than I can count. Sometimes coming home on my own, sometimes getting brought home by the police. I was dealing a lot of Meth and found out I was pregnant. Now what to do? Well, I made the decision to keep the baby, moved back to my mom's, and started attending school on a regular basis again.

I was still doing any drug I could get my hands on everyday. My drug of choice at this time was Meth. I would stay up for days/weeks at a time. I got made to have sex for the first time by my best friend's cousin. I ended up getting expelled my freshman year for drugs and truancy. I started my sophomore year, fourteen and pregnant.

I put my mind to doing well in school again, if not for myself, for my unborn child. I had a really hard pregnancy, complication after complication, and at 32 weeks, went into labor that they couldn't stop it. I remember me and my mom driving around trying to find "Dad," but couldn't. It was an awful feeling. A few hours later, I delivered a 6-pound baby girl. I named her Hunter Miann.

Now, it was a reality that I had to try and get my mind right and my life back together. I did. Over the next several years, I was an awesome mom. I worked at jobs and excelled in school (I graduated at the top of my class), but at the same time I started selling drugs and doing as many as I could get my hands on. I was doing Meth, dropping Acid, and smoking pot on a daily basis. The summer of my senior year, the Drug Enforcement Agency and the drug task force came in for manufacturing Meth. I went to trial. I was 19 years old and scared to death. I won that case—Thank God.

So from this very young age, I felt like two completely different people trapped inside one body.

I moved to Bloomington to attend college but due to my drug use and partying, I only made it one semester and had to move back home. I had quit going to school and quit paying my bills, including my rent and got evicted. I moved back and that again was a smack back to reality—I wanted to do something with my life.

I moved back, got a job, an apartment, and enrolled back in school at Ivy Tech. I fell in love for the first time with a guy named Rusty. I graduated from college with a technical degree in nursing. I was a Licensed Practical Nurse (LPN) and soon after I graduated, I moved in with him. I should say that my addiction was stronger than ever. I felt like if it wasn't for Meth, I wouldn't have made it through school. I was selling more pot and Meth than you can imagine. I was making thousands of dollars a week selling dope and working as a Certified Nursing Assistant (CNA) and going to school full time all the while being a full time mom.

When I moved in with my boyfriend, I quit my job because it was thirty minutes or so away. And besides, me and him were making bank off selling dope. We special ordered new cars, had a nice home, motorcycles, vacations—anything we wanted. We were on top of the world. I had my daughter at my side and a nursing degree. I even paid for a boob job for myself. During this time, I got introduced to Cocaine and prescription pain pills like Oxycontin—I never looked back.

I had without even knowing it been introduced to one of the loves of my life, Oxycontin. The next several years of my life was chaos, fun and excitement. I lived the life of the "picture" dope dealer: vacations, cars, shopping trips, more money than I could spend. It temporarily slowed down when my boyfriend went to jail for selling to an undercover, but we bonded him out for $100,000 full cash only a few weeks later for him to sell to a different undercover.

Now he was set on a million dollar bond, and I had
been to jail and bonded out myself for possession and
withholding information about him. In this short time
frame, he also moved me and my daughter to New
Albany, so I could continue my nursing education and
be okay in life since he was gonna be gone for a while.
I slowed my role for a quick minute because the police
had me scared, and I knew they were watching my
every move. They had even froze all my bank
accounts.

My man was now sentenced to 12 ½ to 25 years for
selling kilos upon kilos and pounds upon pounds to an
undercover, and I was all alone in New Albany.

But the show must go on right? I gave it a few months
for the heat to die down and started dealing and doing
more than ever and started talking to BigN, an old
boyfriend, again.

> Life was crazy as ever
> I had to turn "gangsta" and be shooting at
> people
> Something new cause people wantin' what I
> had
> trying to rob this little girl—

Well, they had a rude awakening. That was my
product, and I was willing to fight and die for it. That
was my livelihood. I ended up moving to Louisville
with BigN. But, I hated it, so I moved back to New
Albany. We had gotten serious, and he asked me to
marry him. He came from money, so I had, for the first
time, been able to put dealing behind me and was
trying to focus on school and "family." We purchased
a beautiful home, drove nice vehicles… life was good?
Not—we fought 24/7, and I still of course used *every
single* day.

My boyfriend, BigN, and I fought 24/7 and I needed
Oxy every single day because I was so unhappy
emotionally and mentally, but for once, I was living a

"normal" life and not wanting for anything financially. So, I toughed it out, got married in 2005, and had my second child in 2006, Olivia Grace.

I graduated from nursing school in 2008 and was now officially a registered nurse (RN). I had two wonderful daughters, a nice house in a nice neighborhood, a good job working labor and delivery at the hospital. Life was good? Not so much. I was miserable at home, out of love, fighting and arguing worse than ever. And in 2007, I lost my little brother and best friend to a car crash. He was only 19—Rest In Peace David Michael. I'm sure this didn't help matters.

I left BigN again and was trying to be in a new relationship. It was a living hell. BigN wanted no one else to have me if he couldn't. Thing was as much as I wanted nothing to do with him, I had to deal with him because we had two young daughters in common. In the time I had left him, he had held me hostage and tried to run me over. He even showed up one day with a pistol threatening me and my new boyfriend.

I went and got my own apartment—signed a one-year lease, and then one day while he was at work, rented a U-Haul, called up some friends, and then I moved out. I had to do it that way because, otherwise, it wouldn't have happened. He would have *never* let me leave. So he came home to find me, the kids, and all our things gone. BOY!

I stayed completely on guard because I knew he was beyond mad. About two months later, just as I had let my guard down a little, I walked out of my apartment to leave. He was waiting in his car across the parking lot and was coming full speed ahead. He had all intentions of taking me out completely. I somehow got out of dodge just in time. My oldest daughter seen it happen and called 911 without me even knowing. But he was long gone by the time the police showed up, and I didn't pursue any charges. That would have just made things even worse.

I had worked all night the next night, a 7 pm to 7 am shift, and was headed an hour away to my hometown to get away for a couple days and had my youngest daughter with me. BigN had called, and we were arguing like no other over the phone while I was driving. So, I was paying no attention and lost control of my SUV and flipped over the guardrail and flipped over and over again down a huge ravine—finally a tree stump stopped us. We were upside down with all our doors and windows jammed. The ambulance couldn't find us because we had flipped so far down the hillside. So, I finally got the windshield kicked out and climbed out with my baby to the top.

After that, I started talking to someone new—fell head over heels in love— well lust— and got remarried in 2010 to Jon Roll.

So one day I sat down with both of them, Jon and BigN, and made it clear that they were doing nothing but making my life hell, not to mention the kids. Well lo and behold, they went from trying to kill each other to them becoming best friends and wanting to hang out together all the time. Go figure.

When the baby was about three months old, my ex-husband (BigN) and his girlfriend moved in with me and my husband because they had nowhere else to go, no money, and was really bad off on drugs. I told them they could stay in my basement until they got on their feet. Bad choice--my ex hit on me every chance he got and was getting my current husband to take off with him on binges.

I would have to track them down or just wait on them to come back home. The last straw was they stole my car because his truck was out of gas, and they left me with no car, no money, dope sick, and with all the kids. UGH! For days I couldn't get a ride to go find them counties away, and they wouldn't answer their phones. Remember, I was broke.

So I finally said, "Fuck it!" I came up with $3,800, a

ride, and wasn't dope sick anymore. So me and my ex-husband's girlfriend went and got my car back. Long story short, we did, and we left the boys stranded several counties away.

My systems caught in a conniption,

my stomachs all in knots,

feining for my medicine.

It consumes my every thought,

to get myself together I work up the next shot.

First steps admittin',

nah, the first step is quitin'.

I got a problem, and I need some help.

I need you by my side. I can't do this by myself.

I almost feel I can't be cured,

rehab don't want me cause I ain't insured.

I done been like this for way too long,

searchin' for a prayer askin' God to bring me home.

I shut the life and my lite out, I wanna be alone.

Things just spiraled further and further out of control very quickly after this. I wasn't working. I was drawing unemployment, but that wasn't nearly enough to support myself, my husband, and my three kids. It was the start of summer and already very hot, and I had no electricity and no way to pay it to turn it back on and no money for my car and house payment. I was very behind and had had to place the kids with grandparents, and the oldest with a friend.

Once again my life had become unmanageable and my addiction was out of control. The end of June, we moved fifty miles away, back to our hometown of Brownstown and moved in with Jon's parents so I could save up my unemployment and get a place back home so I would have help with the kids. I got a duplex by the end of July and got a job as an RN at a local nursing home. At this point, I was still abusing Meth, but had laid the Opiates down. But, I was now around lots of narcotics twelve hours a day. This is a Bad, Bad Thing for Valerie.

I started back up on Opiates and within a matter of weeks was out of control on Opiates again and stealing twenty to over a hundred of them a night from my place of employment. My relationship with my husband had been on the brinks for some time. He just quit coming home except to shit, shower, or shave. I had, had enough, and I kicked him out.

Now remember BigN? Well, of course he has never quit trying to be with me so as soon as he caught word that I had kicked Jon out, he took full advantage of the situation. His addiction was out of control, and he was shooting any and everything and had been for a few years. He wanted to spend the night, so he could take the girls to their first day of school. I ended up agreeing. And well, long story short—he never left. I, like an idiot, only encouraged his drug use. I wasn't only stealing pills and supporting his Meth habit, I was bringing him hundreds of clean needles home every night. My reasoning was: "Well, at least this way I know he's using a clean needle every time, so it's okay."

He had a tray he kept all his paraphernalia on, and he kept it up in the top of the bathroom closet. Well my oldest daughter and her friend went to get something out the closet one day and his tray fell down. No one knew this event occurred until it was too late. The friend went home and of course told her mom, and the mom called Child Protective Services (CPS). I came home from work one day and my house was empty and there was a card from CPS on the door. Come to find out that while I was at work and they were at school, CPS had taken them and placed them with their grandparents for emergency placement.

I LOST IT. MY WORLD HAD JUST COMPLETELY FALLEN APART. I never looked back. I quit my job and started shooting drugs, a whole new level of addiction for me. I was 29 years old at this point. I quit caring about anyone (including myself) or anything. I loved that high more than myself from the first time I shot up. By late November, I was careless, homeless, and kidless. Over the next 3 and a half years, it was complete chaos at all times. I lived in and out of county jails, prisons, cars, trap houses, and you know, wherever.

I remember being incarcerated one time. I got bonded out for $3,000. I was so dope sick that I never missed a beat. I did a shot literally within thirty seconds of being released. BigN got the money to bond me out. That arrest was in Scott County, and I had ran from the police and caught myself several charges, seven in all and most of them felonies. So I was out on bond in January and was at a friend's house, actually hiding out from BigN. I had just got back from picking up a bunch of Heroin from Cincinnati when the police came bum rushing in. Thank God I had just got it all bagged up and was able to stuff it. But they found needles and paraphernalia in the house, so we all went to jail. On a lighter note, best jail stay ever because I had 4 g's of Heroin stuffed. I went in on a Friday and got released on my own recognizance on a Monday. So, I stayed high as hell during my whole jail stay. Fuck You, Dope Sickness.

A couple of friends picked me up at a gas station, down the road from the jail. We went about ten minutes away, and I got more Heroin and never missed a beat. This freedom was again short lived. I didn't know I had a warrant out of Jackson County.

On February 23, my oldest daughter's 16th birthday, I got arrested. So I sat there until April. At that time, BigN's mom had filed my taxes for me, and I got almost $11,000 back, so I bonded myself out for $3,500. I went straight to Scott County where he was locked up and bonded him out for $4,500. The few grand I had left, of course, all went to our habit. So now, I am out on bond in three counties and have $11,000 cash wrapped up in bonds.

I was out of Jackson County a whole four days and then went back to Clark County on a warrant for failure to appear. I was only there a couple of weeks, just had to wait on the courts to work me in to their dockets. They O-Red me or released me on my own recognizance, because I was locked up in another county which was why I failed to appear. I stayed out a couple months and after a crazy blackout, I got arrested by the state police for a possession of hypodermic (needle charge) and once again went back to jail June 20, 2014. So, now I had two cases in Scott County. The state wrapped all my stuff together, and I sat until September 27, 2014 and left with time served and 18 months probation. I had another court date for Jackson County in December of 2014. It was my sentencing hearing, and I had signed a blind plea so was looking at either no jail time to up to three years. It was completely up to the judge. Did I go to sentencing? No. GRRRR… now yet another warrant.

Now let me tell you that having all these warrants is completely exhausting. I was always looking over my back, having to dodge the police at *all* times. It really takes a toll on ya. I would show up at someone's house usually only to find out the police had already been there looking for me. Crazy thing though, I ended up living right under their nose—directly across from the courthouse and jail above a bar in an apartment. They finally got a tip, and I had to jump out a really tall window. I got away though. Then I was partying one night at a hotel, and the police came for "suspected drug activity". I had nowhere to run, so once again, jail here I come. This was March 14, 2014.

I got released on August 4 from Rockville, but had holds for Clark County for another failure to appear and Scott County for a failure to appear and a probation violation. Ugh! I went to court for Clark County and signed a plea to eighteen months probation and got released to Scott County. They released me and gave me court dates for my probation violation. I was chillin' at a friend's and here came the police bustin' in, so I went to jail for my P.T.R., and a new possession charge and visiting a common nuisance possession. This was in February 2015. I thought I was going back to prison and at the last minute, they agreed to rehab. So, on May 14, 2015 on my daughter's 9th birthday, I entered the doors of Wheeler Mission, court ordered and two years on the shelf.

Crazy Highs

I don't remember even half the real crazy ones. It's amazing how, as I sit sober and look back on life, just how much of it is a complete blur.

How sad. Life is so short, and most of mine I can't even remember.

So forewarning, unless you have lived this, it will probably sound like nonsense to you, but to me all these crazy-chaotic highs and falsehoods or whatever you want to call them were oh so real to me.

It's amazing really what drugs can do to your brain. It's Total and Complete Insanity. You know the definition of insanity—doing the same things over and over expecting a different result—that never comes—I was the definition of Insane.

Remember as you are reading that all these events are fiction but this is what I thought was happening. I'm sorry if this is hard for to understand as you are reading. It's hard for me to write it to make sense…. because it was nonsense.

One night my boyfriend was rescuing kids from the police because they were trying to drown them in the creek thinking people were after us and chasing us to the point of putting ourselves and others in danger. Thinking there were snipers outside, taking all the closet and inside doors off the hinges to cover all the windows so they couldn't get or to see in. Going on fake high-speed chases because we thought berries and cherries were chasing us. Instead of driving our car, we were pushing it around town at 2 to 3 a.m. in the morning, because if we drove it they (whoever they was) would hear us. My ex laying on the clothes dryer in a fetal position eating a lemon to the point of launching it like a hand grenade and repeating this for hours and hours. Just complete and utter paranoia, voices in your head that never stop.

I could go on but I think you see the idea. I did this to myself for years and years. Sometimes I would cry and cry and feel like that was the time I had done it and took drug use so far that I would never be "normal" again. I've blacked out several times to come to hours and hours (longest one was 18 hours) later and not remember even being blacked out. I've overdosed three times, and once I was by myself. Four and half hours later, I somehow came to, face down in the mud in the woods in the pouring rain. Waking up or coming to countless times with dried blood everywhere and a needle still hanging out of my arm or right next to me somewhere because I was doing such big shots of usually Opana/Heroine. I even messed with Meth a lot (speed-balling), and I would be out before I could even get the whole shot pushed in. I would wake up or come to, whatever you call it, and without even hesitating, do the rest of the shot.

The needle is my number one weakness even more so than the drugs in it. It consumed my every thought. Sometimes I would poke myself just to see the flash of blood in the needle—that, in itself, was a high for me. At my lowest point, I was doing a shot at least every two hours in 24 hours a day and sometimes shots in between those two hours. I had destroyed all my veins in my hands, arms, legs, breasts, so I went to my neck. I now have a huge scar on the right side of my neck because I got a miss and had to have surgery on it. I was so strung out that even in my entire hospital stay of six days, I used my IV site to shoot up every couple hours. I was doing thousands of dollars of drugs all day, every day as long as I wasn't in jail.

How did I afford it? Pretty self-explanatory by now; I dealt them. I cared about myself and only myself – I distanced myself from everyone including my mom, my kids, every and anybody that wasn't in my drug circle.

Vanity = Self
Indulgence = Valerie

Remember like I said earlier, the needle and the drugs was the only thing I thought or cared about. I had met the love of my life or so I thought. In actuality, I had met Mr. Diablo himself.

My Trials

Well like most people I have had one trial after another. It all started before I even knew what trials were. When I was three and a half years old, I lost my dad to cancer, and in a sense, lost my mom too. Preschool was a trial I never did conquer. It conquered me. I threw such fits and disliked it so much that my mom let me stop going.

Kindergarten wasn't much better. It was probably three months or so before I finally got comfortable. After that though, I excelled in school and even got to skip the third grade.

My next set of trials came during my sixth grade summer. I was introduced to drugs, and that is a trial I have struggled with to present day.

Another huge trial was getting pregnant at fourteen years old and deciding to keep the baby. It was a very hard decision. She in now going to be a college freshman in the fall double majoring in performing arts and psychology. I'm so very proud of her.

Her father and my ex-husband was and still is an ongoing trial in my life and will be for at least the next nine years because our second daughter won't be eighteen for nine more years.

Getting my nursing license suspended after years of hard work and dedication in getting my degree. Of all of my arrests (I have had 9 in all I think), most were felony convictions.

Losing my grandparents a few winters ago was hard. They gave me what little upbringing I had. I lost them both within a few months of each other. When I showed up at my grandpa's funeral, my family wouldn't even let me in, because I looked so bad, and I was so fucked up.

I lost my best friend and brother to a car wreck in 2007, and we had to have a closed casket because he was burnt alive and had to be identified by his dental records.

Going into labor with my second daughter six weeks early and six hours away from home at a baby shower. I made it to the hospital in the nick of time.

Being hooked on drugs with my last pregnancy. Agreeing to sign my rights over of my youngest child and my only son to his parental grandparents.

Losing everything I had worked so hard for: houses, cars, Harleys, ATV's, etc.

Losing everyone I loved and cared for.

Too many acid trips, Ecstasy binges, constant Methamphetamine and Opiate use. Being a needle junkie. Overdoses, misses from IV drug use, which required surgery

160

A tubal pregnancy, where I died on the table.

Totaling multiple vehicles.

Being homeless….Being at beyond rock bottom.

Meeting my soul mate, Brian, (we been together since October 2013) and now having to be apart from him. I'm in rehab at a homeless shelter, and he's incarcerated.

All these trials and so many more I neglected to mention have only made the person I am. I will prevail. I will come out on top—Believe that!

What Have I Lost?

- My Dad
- My little brother
- My sanity at times
- My career (My nursing license was revoked)
- My home
- My car
- My "real" friends
- My freedom (jail and prison stays)
- All maternal things

What I Haven't Lost?

- My self-respect
- My positive attitude
- My Mom (always there for me)
- My smile
- Myself

The End

As I sit on my bed in rehab, I look back and really the only word that comes to mind is: WOW.
I truly can't believe I'm still here to tell my story. I have lived a very crazy life. I have made a lot of big mistakes. I have hurt a lot of people including myself, but I honestly don't regret anything.

Everything happens for a reason, and life always works out in the end just as God intended it to. I now have an awesome relationship with my mom and kids. I've made some really awesome sober friends and laugh and smile all day, every day. It's great to be able to enjoy life as much as I do now (and even remember it all, completely sober.)

If you would have asked me five months ago if I would ever be where I am at now, I would have laughed at you and probably even told you to go fuck yourself. I know sobriety will be a lifelong battle, but with good people a good attitude and God, I have the upper hand on addiction. I hope you enjoyed reading my memoirs, and that it touched your heart. I will end by one of favorite quotes by Aldous Huxley, " Experience is not what happens to a man; it is what a man does with what happens to him."

Barbara McLaughlin, Volunteer
Valerie, The Storyteller

I'm sitting inside Wheeler Mission listening as beautiful, smart, courageous, wounded women read their stories about opiate use and an addiction that has cost them dearly. Their words are powerful, rife with sordid details, street talk, humor, regret, pain, and gratitude. I marvel—as they do—that they're still around. Most thank God and say He must have a purpose for their lives.

I agree with them.

Valerie's stories read like movie scripts—high speed car chases, jail time, cops busting down doors. Some of her antics sound funny, and you can't help but laugh with her, until you stop and think of all that she's lost. She writes that she used to be an RN before she got her license revoked. She wouldn't go back to nursing anyway, she says. Too much of a temptation with all the drugs around. She talks about a drug called Opana that got her into trouble, mentions that warrants were out for her in Scott and Clark counties before she came here. I take it all in, but that particular drug and those counties mean nothing to me; I've never heard of them.

A few days later, I'm at home, glancing at the newspaper. A headline reads: **Another county may request needle exchange.** I scan the article, and, sure enough, the counties mentioned are Scott and Clark—Valerie's counties. I read that there's an HIV and hepatitis C outbreak linked to needle sharing among people who inject a liquefied form of the painkiller Opana. Though I've never heard Valerie mention sharing needles, HIV, or Hepatitis C, she has become the face of those counties for me. She may have nothing in common with the average drug addict in Southern Indiana. But her toned and tan and tattooed arm is the one I picture at the end of a dirty needle when I read that article again. Suddenly, the statistics, the need to declare a state health epidemic, the request for a needle exchange program strike me as important and alarming. We have to do something. Beautiful, smart, courageous, wounded lives are on the line!

I thank God that Valerie is still at Wheeler and getting help. I marvel at her writing ability, and I'll always be grateful to her for opening my eyes. I pray for her and the other women. *Please, God, give them the strength to hold on.* I worry about the ones who've written brilliant, hopeful, cautionary tales and then disappear from the program. As a fiction writer, I like my characters' stories to end on a high note. Lessons learned. Strife overcome. But I've discovered that these real life tales of addiction often repeat themselves.

My personal plea for Valerie: Hang on to your pen. Cross out the lies. Write your best story—one word at a time—and don't let the bad guy win. Keep up the good fight, Valerie, because your life is worth it.

Editor and Artist Biographies

Darolyn "Lyn" Jones is passionate about literacy in and out of the classroom. Lyn co-created the Memoir Project with Barbara Shoup at the Indiana Writers Center and now oversees that program as the Education Outreach Director. Lyn is also the author of the popular educational text, *Painless Reading Comprehension*, the editor of the digital literary magazine, *Rethinking Children's Literature*, an editor with INwords Publications, and the editor of seven different memoir collections. Her scholarly publications about both community writing and disability studies have appeared in a variety of peer-reviewed academic journals. In addition to the Indiana Writers Center, Lyn is also a professor in the Department of English at Ball State University.

Student Editor Rita D. Mitchell is a student at Ball State University currently serving as President of the Alliance of Black Teachers, and Co-Treasurer of the English Education Club. She plans to graduate in spring of 2016 with her Bachelor's degree in English/Language Arts Education. She desires to teach in her hometown until she return's to graduate school to earn her doctorial degree. When she is not working or studying, you can find her spending time with family and friends, listening to music, or getting lost in the pages of a good book.

Technical Editor Michael Baumann earned his MA in Rhetoric and Composition at Ohio University. He currently teaches composition at the University of Louisville while pursuing a PhD in English. Michael has edited, designed, and produced seven other anthologies of public memoir with the Indiana Writers Center.

Student Editor Elisabeth (Niki) Wilkes is a recent Ball State University graduate who is now working on getting a degree in Publishing Studies at the University College London, in the hopes of being able to bring stories that need to be heard to the reading world. She especially loves true and heartfelt stories about overcoming hardships. Some of her favorites include *The Glass Castle, Fun Home,* and *Confessions of a Mega Church Pastor.*

Volunteer Editor Jessica Mayo - Schwab is a reader, writer, and a social worker. She holds a BA in English from Indiana University and a MSW from IUPUI. When she's not fighting for social justice, she can be found hiking along the Monon trail, herding her three cats, or sampling the local fare with her husband.

Volunteer Editor Barbara McLaughlin is a journalist, novelist, and children's book author. Her picture book, *Reuben Rides the Rails*, was a Christamore House selected book in 2010. She began her career in sports writing and has traveled the world with U.S. Olympic and national diving teams. A former Indiana Writers Center board member, she enjoys running marathons and finds qualifying for Boston easier than getting her novels published.

Cover Artist Andrea Boucher is currently earning her MFA in the Butler University Creative Writing program. After building a career in the corporate world as an editor and technical writer for various companies, she decided to do what she really wanted in life, which is to be a nonfiction writer who moonlights as a book designer. She has done numerous covers for the Indiana Writers Center and makes it no secret that these are her favorite projects.

Photographer Giovanna Mandel is a family and high school senior photographer living in Zionsville, Indiana. She spent the first part of her life as a "Jersey" girl. She headed to the Midwest to follow the love of her life and became an elementary school teacher. She is a mom to two terrific young men and spends her winters exploring Arizona with her husband. http://www.amiciphotography.com

Acknowledgments

The Indiana Writers Center and INwords Publications wishes to gratefully acknowledge the support of these organizations and individuals who helped make this project possible and this book a reality.

Barbara Shoup, Executive Director of the Indiana Writers Center

Darolyn "Lyn" Jones, Education Outreach Director, Indiana Writers Center, Editor, INwords Publications

Laura Bays, Volunteer Coordinator for Wheeler Mission Ministries Center for Women and Children

Rita D. Mitchell, Ball State University English Education Student and Teaching and Editing Intern for the Indiana Writers Center

Michael Baumann, University of Louisville English Doctoral Student and Book Designer and Editor for the INwords Publications at the Indiana Writers Center

Nikki Wilkes, University College London Professional Writing Graduate Student and Editing Intern for the Indiana Writers Center

Volunteers Barbara Kazanjian,Tracy Line, Jessica Mayo, Barbara McLaughlin, Mary Lynn Moore, Jen Noelle, Alicia Pattison, & Rachel Sahaidachny - - thank you for volunteering countless hours writing with the women and transcribing their works.

Laurel Fassold for supplying wonderful home baked food.

Giovanna "Joanne" Mandel for your time and beautiful photos that truly capture the beauty and spirit of these women.

Andrea Boucher for your time and continued commitment in creating such beautiful covers that capture the words inside.

A very special thank you to the Allen Whitehill Clowes Charitable Foundation, Inc. in Indianapolis whose funding made this project possible.

We wish to thank all of the individual donors who contributed to our Power2Give site and helped make this book possible.

Finally and most importantly, for the women of Wheeler who had the courage to speak and write their truths about becoming homeless and for giving a face and a voice to homelessness.

If you would like more information about Wheeler or how you can assist Wheeler with their mission, visit their website at www.wheelermission.org

For additional information on how you can help the homeless, visit http://wheelermission.org/learn-more/ways-to-help-a-homeless-person/

For more information about the Indiana Writers Center, visit www.indianawriters.org

For more information about our outreach programming and the Memoir Project, visit http://www.indianawriters.org/pages/outreach